T0358119

Paul B. Kidd is a Sydney-based author, photo-journalist, magazine editor, Radio 2UE broadcaster and freelance *60 Minutes* researching producer who specialises in true crime, big-game fishing, humour and adventure.

Paul's articles, interviews and photographs have appeared in most Australian major outdoors and men's publications and in numerous magazines and websites worldwide.

Paul B. Kidd is a recognised authority on Australian serial killers and criminals who have been sentenced to life imprisonment, never to be released.

Paul is the author of ten books and lives in Sydney's eastern suburbs with his partner Jenny.

NEVER TO BE RELEASED

PAUL B. KIDD

PAN
Pan Macmillan Australia

First published 1993 by Pan Macmillan Australia Pty Limited
This Pan edition published 2001 by Pan Macmillan Australia Pty Limited
1 Market St, Sydney

Reprinted 2001, 2002, 2003, 2004, 2005, 2006, 2007, 2008, 2009

National Library of Australia
cataloguing-in-publication data:

Kidd, Paul B. (Paul Benjamin), 1945–.
Never to be released.

ISBN 978 0 330 36293 1 (pbk.).

1. Violent crimes – Australia. 2. Criminals – Australia
3. Murder – Australia – Case studies. 1. Title

364.10994

Typeset in Times Roman by Post Pre-press Group
Printed by IVE

To the legendary crime reporter, the late Joe Morris. He may be gone, but the legend lives on.

Foreword

This is a book about violent crime.

I grew up with crime stories. My father, Joe Morris, was a police rounds reporter for a major metropolitan newspaper. Each night when he arrived home my mother would ask the question wives would traditionally ask: 'How'd it go today, dear?' His reply was never anything quite so simple as having lost or obtained the Jones account. His stories dealt with death. And sometimes one look at his taut features told the story that there had been more than one victim that day.

In those days, I never gave much significance to what I was hearing. Some childhood memories...

The headless and handless corpse propped up against a tree.

The woman who put her baby in the oven.

The boy who shot and killed his mother

because she had said *he* was being naughty.

The mother who hacked her two children to death. The devil told her to do it.

The man who raped the young black girl... after he strangled and stabbed her.

The next-door neighbour who shot the family of five and the family goat.

It would be fair to say that crime dominated my father's life. And, perhaps the most terrible of all crimes, murder became his major interest. And his major fear. As Marlon Brando said in *Apocalypse Now*. 'The horror, the horror'.

My father saw too many victims. He developed an almost irrational fear and horror of those he loved being harmed. But was it so irrational? He knew that your life could change if you failed to lock the front door. He had seen the dead on the floor to prove it. He knew that the innocent act of picking up a hitchhiker could end with a knife plunged into your heart. And he also knew that your kiddie wasn't quite as safe as you might believe walking to the corner store or playing in the park. After all, he'd been one of the first on the scene when their bodies had been found.

'Joey, take great care. I couldn't stand it if anything happened to you,' was his usual farewell as I headed for the door.

Even when I was young, this struck me as being somewhat selfish. *He* couldn't stand it... what about me?

I realise now that my father knew something

that I didn't. The dead are dead. Perhaps the people who suffer the most are those who, in his words, are 'left to carry on'. There is usually more than one victim of violent crime and sometimes there is a chain of victims whose lives are altered forever.

We talk about the suffering of families whose treasured ones are torn from them by violent crime. But I'm not so sure we give full credit to the real suffering they endure. Do we really know how the father feels when he has to identify his dead child? What goes through the mind of a mother when she gives court evidence of the last time she saw her daughter alive... with the killer watching impassively, or maybe even smirking, from a few metres away? How does the family feel when the horrific facts are told and then retold in at least one committal hearing and a further trial? Never mind the prospect of the appeals courts.

And finally, how do families feel when the person who has virtually destroyed their lives is eventually sentenced? Families have seen killers given everything from good behaviour bonds to sentences of life imprisonment. But what about life sentences?

Most families, like everybody else, realise that life doesn't mean *life*. What it does mean is a period of time influenced and determined by politicians, parole boards, counsellors, social workers, ministers of religion, lobby groups, prison warders, lawyers and the killer himself or herself.

Too many families have seen killers freed to kill again. So did my father. He would have been more than happy to kill most, if not all of them. He saw the horror they created. But he was also a pragmatist. So when killers were told they were 'never to be released' he obtained some small satisfaction.

My father felt that the actions of the worst killers should be remembered. And if he had his way, made mandatory reading for all those people whose positions could influence leniency. Paul B. Kidd and my father were starting on this book when my father died. Paul has finished it.

Throughout the writing of *Never to be Released* I had the privilege of being asked to assist with the editing. On many days I sat down to help describe in simple terms how people stabbed, raped, garrotted, shot, strangled, sodomised or otherwise brutalised their fellow human beings. And each night I had violent and ugly nightmares. Paul B. Kidd had recurring dreams of death throughout the entire writing of this book.

Yet Paul and I weren't really involved in any of this tragedy. We were simply observers, writers trained to be objective. But we too experienced the horror. Similarly, you will find that you can't read this book and remain objective. Please God, let us hope that it helps keep

these killers where they should be, locked away
for the rest of their lives, never to be released.

JOSEPH MORRIS
MAY 1992

(Joseph Morris (Jnr) is the director of the Australian College
of Journalism and Principal of the Australian News
Syndicate.)

Contents

Contents

Acknowledgements

This book has been compiled with the assistance of my wife Jennifer, the late Joe Morris, Joe Morris Jnr, Simon Townsend, Samantha and Michael Oliver and Peter Olszewski.

The newspapers around Australia have been superb. My many thanks to David Taylor at the *West Australian*, Brian Branigan at the *Courier-Mail* in Brisbane, Lurline Campbell at News Ltd in Sydney, and the library staff at the *Adelaide Advertiser* and the Melbourne *Age*. And a special thankyou to the ladies with the photos at News Ltd, Elaine Saunders and Del Courtenay. Thanks also to the courteous staff at the Mitchell Library in Sydney.

While the departments of Corrective Services around the country are reluctant to part with any information, the public relations departments in Sydney and Brisbane have been of wonderful assistance without breaking any of the rules. Thanks to Bob Stapleton in Sydney and Roger Pladstow and Roger Carstens in Brisbane.

Introduction

There is no such prison sentence as 'never to be released'. It is merely a recommendation by someone in authority, usually a judge, that the prisoner shall go to gaol and die there. This recommendation is reserved for the most dastardly of criminals. The child murderers. Those who rape and murder in packs. The mass murderers. The serial killers.

The recommendation that a prisoner never be released is not one that is taken lightly. Every murderer in this book is still in prison. At the time of writing one had been there for thirty-two years. Another for thirty. Their crimes are so horrific that it is inconceivable that any one of them could ever be allowed back into society.

Prior to the abolition of the death penalty in the 1960s, these types of murderers were sentenced to die on the gallows, though few of them did. Most had their sentences commuted to 'life imprisonment', which usually meant a minimum of fourteen years behind bars.

There was also another term used in those days, called 'at the governor's pleasure'. This meant that the prisoner would be gaoled without a term of imprisonment being set. In other words, if the governor of the time saw fit to let the prisoner go, usually on the recommendation of a parole board, then the prisoner would be set free. However, this method of sentencing was reserved for the most heinous of villains and few, if any, were ever released. Apart from the death penalty, it was the most feared of all sentences. The recommendation that a prisoner never be released is a near equivalent to the 'governor's pleasure'.

To be best of my knowledge, the first time that the term 'never to be released' was used was in 1962, when the then New South Wales Minister for Justice, Mr N. J. Mannix, made the notation on the sentencing papers of the sex-killer, Lenny Lawson. Mannix wrote: 'While appreciating that I cannot bind the hand of any future Executive Government, I am strongly of the view that Leonard Keith Lawson should never be released'. Lenny Lawson is still in prison.

Since then the term has been used only sparingly. It is a recommendation reserved for only the worst imaginable crimes, usually when judges or psychiatrists feel so strongly about a case that they insist that their opinion never be forgotten. In one of the most recent cases, the judge insisted that the murderers of Anita Cobby have their papers clearly marked 'never to be released'. One hopes this would have some influence on a future parole board in keeping the killers behind bars forever.

Surprisingly, other killers found guilty of the most ghastly crimes have been sentenced to life imprisonment without the 'never to be released' recommendation. They include:

Julian Knight, the Hoddle Street murderer, who killed seven people and wounded nineteen others when he opened fire on motorists and pedestrians at Clifton Hill in suburban Melbourne in August 1987. Knight was sentenced in the Victorian Supreme Court to life imprisonment with a minimum parole period of twenty-eight years.

The Russell Street bombers, Stanley Brian Taylor and Craig John Minogue. The Victorian Supreme Court sentenced Taylor to life with no fixed parole period and Minogue to life with a minimum of twenty-eight years for planting a car full of explosives out the front of the Russell Street Police Station, Melbourne, in March 1986. A young policewoman was killed in the explosion.

Berwyn Rees, who in August 1977 murdered a Bondi Junction gun shop proprietor and a customer, then shot and killed a police officer during his arrest for the murders, three years later. In the New South Wales Supreme Court, Rees was sentenced to life imprisonment.

Anthony Gerald Sebastian Lanigan, who cold-bloodedly murdered a young female opal courier, Norelle Grogan, in 1977, while on parole after serving half of a fourteen-year sentence for manslaughter. Lanigan was sentenced to life in the New South Wales Supreme Court.

Stephen Leslie Bradley, who in 1960 kidnapped and murdered eight-year-old Graham Thorne from Bondi only weeks after the boy's parents had won first prize in the Opera House Lottery. Sentenced to life imprisonment in the New South Wales Supreme Court, Bradley died in Goulburn gaol in 1968.

It is highly unlikely that any of these surviving killers will be freed, but it was not recommended that they never be released by the sentencing judge or by psychiatrists.

'Never to be released' is so rare a recommendation that the majority of the cases in Australia where it has been applied are in this book. However, I may well have missed some. With a couple of exceptions, the Corrective Services departments in most States are uncooperative and reluctant to give any information about their inmates.

In a rare case, a prisoner has inflicted the penalty on himself. Convicted murderer, James Miller, received six life terms for his part in the infamous Truro murders in South Australia. Miller has no hope of ever being freed as he has never asked for a period to be set when he will be eligible to apply for parole. Although Miller vehemently denies murdering anyone, he accepts that his part in the crimes was so serious that he will never be released.

Releasing any of the murderers in this book would be the equivalent of setting Charles Manson or the Yorkshire Ripper loose. There would be a public outcry, no matter how much the prisoner had been rehabilitated. The murderers in this book are among the most despicable in the world. Even writing about them has been a nightmare. These past few months I have gone to bed night after night with different atrocities inside my head. My days of research have been filled with violent deaths, rape, brutality and almost indescribable horror.

I have had to get up and walk away from my research many times, for fear of being ill. I have suffered fits of depression, anger and hatred. Yet it is impossible for me to imagine how the victims must have felt, or their parents, relatives and loved ones must still feel.

Although I have always been fascinated with crime, writing about it as a career was never my intention. I am a magazine editor, television and radio presenter and freelance photo/journalist. I like to write about fishing, the outdoors and comedy. All the fun things in life. So how did I get involved with the most infamous killers this country has known?

A few years back I teamed up with Joe

Morris, the legendary police rounds reporter who had been following the cops around to the most horrific crimes for nearly half a century. Joe had covered all of the famous cases. The Thorne kidnapping, the Bogle–Chandler murders, the Mutilator murders and the Wanda Beach murders are just a few that come to mind. Joe was a walking encyclopaedia of horror.

With my enthusiasm and Joe's extraordinary knowledge, we decided to do a book together. But most of the crimes had been done to death, so to speak. Joe's wealth of experience with criminals who had been put away forever gave us an insight into just who was in prison for the rest of their lives. This book is the result.

Joe had a hatred for people like the ones you will read about in this book. He despised the vermin who force themselves upon defenceless women and children. He loathed the bullies and cowards who hunt in packs, preying on the weak and the innocent. He abhorred those who expose themselves in public and flaunt their sexual preferences in sleazy bars. Joe Morris was a man's man.

The unequalled horrors of the Mutilator murders, as told in this book, were taken straight from the story told by the Mutilator himself. Joe Morris interviewed William Mac-Donald at length in his cell at Long Bay gaol. At huge personal risk of being discovered by both the Mutilator and the authorities, Morris recorded every word of the interview on a hidden tape-recorder. Until now, the full inside story of Australia's only mutilation serial killings, has never been told.

It was Joe Morris who wrote the story of the extraordinary capture of the Mutilator. His story was tagged with what now is probably the best remembered crime headline of our times, 'The Case of The Walking Corpse'.

The book was almost at the writing stage when Joe had a stroke and died a week before Christmas, 1991. A lot of the research had been done and I decided to go ahead by myself. Old Joe might have been gone, but he certainly wasn't forgotten. His name opened a lot of doors for me. If I rang a newspaper for a bit of difficult information, I would drop Joe Morris' name and nothing was a problem any more. He was a legend in the newspaper business. It was as if Joe had been looking after the project. As if he were still here.

His son, journalist Joe Morris Jnr, has been of invaluable assistance to me in the editing and structuring of the book. Without his help, the project would have taken a lot longer. Joe Morris Jnr kindly wrote the foreword. I wouldn't have dreamed of asking anyone else.

My wife Jennifer, who helped so much with the research at libraries, had a lot to put up with during the writing of this book.

I used to have mixed feelings on capital

punishment. But after the hundreds of hours spent researching this book, I firmly believe that all sex murderers and child killers should be put to death.

Let us pray that the governments of the future heed the advice of the judges and psychiatrists of the past. Let's hope that they keep these criminals where they belong. Behind bars. Caged, like the beasts that they are. Never to be Released.

PAUL B. KIDD
SYDNEY 1992

1 The Case of the Walking Corpse

As William MacDonald — dubbed 'the Mutilator' — was testifying how he stabbed one of his victims in the neck thirty times and then removed the man's testicles and penis with the same knife, a woman in the jury fainted. Justice McLennan stopped the proceedings and excused the juror from the rest of the grisly evidence. He then ordered MacDonald to continue.

The gallery listened in awe as the Mutilator told of the killings in great detail. He explained how the blood had sprayed all over his raincoat as he castrated his victims, put their private parts in a plastic bag and took them home. He also told the jury what he did with the genitals when he arrived back at his lodgings.

With the conviction of William MacDonald, the horrors of what had become known as the Mutilator murders came to a close. The Mutilator was Australia's first true serial killer and investigating police had no trouble in connecting the murders he committed to an unknown psychopath. The Mutilator's crimes were easily recognised. His victims were always derelicts. They had been violently stabbed to death. All had their genitals cut off.

But catching the Mutilator was no easy task. William MacDonald was as elusive as he was barbaric, and in the end it was only a freak incident that brought him to justice. 'The Case of the Walking Corpse', as one newspaper headline dubbed it, is one of the most bizarre cases in Australian criminal history.

William MacDonald was born in Liverpool, England, in 1924, the middle of three children. In 1943, at the age of nineteen, he joined the army and was transferred to the Lancashire Fusiliers. One night MacDonald was raped in an air-raid shelter by a corporal, who threatened MacDonald with death if he told anyone.

At first the young private felt bad about what had happened, but as time went by he realised he had enjoyed the experience. MacDonald claimed that this was the start of his life as a homosexual. Being raped by that corporal would be constantly on MacDonald's mind as he murdered and mutilated his victims in years to come.

Years before his killing rampage, MacDonald became an active homosexual, soliciting men in public toilets and bars. His obvious homosexuality made life difficult in those conservative times and he moved from job to job as the taunts and ridicule became too much for him to cope.

In 1947, William MacDonald consulted a psychiatrist about his mental condition, complaining that the persecution was causing illusions and strange noises in his head. At the psychiatrist's recommendation, he spent the next three months in a mental institution. But it changed nothing.

When he came out of the institution, Mac-Donald decided that if he couldn't change his life he could change countries. He emigrated to Canada in 1949 and then to Australia in 1955 where, shortly after his arrival, he was charged with indecent assault when he touched a detective on the penis in a public toilet in Adelaide. MacDonald was placed on a two-year good behaviour bond.

MacDonald moved to Ballarat, but trouble seemed to follow him around. While he was working on a construction site, his workmates gave him a hiding for being a 'poofter'. Mac-Donald bought a very sharp knife and slashed the tyres of their bicycles.

Moving from state to state, MacDonald held jobs only until the taunts became so strong he had to move on. All of the time the urge to kill his tormentors was building up in him. It seemed that everywhere he went, people would talk about him and make fun of him behind his back. He was completely paranoid.

The murders began in Brisbane in 1960. Mac-Donald befriended fifty-five-year-old Amos Hurst outside the Roma Street Railway Station. They had a long drinking session in a hotel together and went back to Hurst's hotel room, where they sat on the bed and drank beer.

Hurst was so drunk that he probably had no idea that MacDonald was strangling him until it was too late. MacDonald claimed that he had no intentions of murdering Hurst when they went back to his room. But the urge to kill him came on suddenly and he squeezed tightly.

As he was being strangled, Amos Hurst had haemorrhaged and blood poured from his mouth all over MacDonald's hands. Mac-Donald punched him in the face and Hurst fell to the floor dead.

MacDonald then undressed Hurst and put him into bed. He washed the blood from his arms, quietly left the building and returned to his lodgings in South Brisbane.

William MacDonald looked in the papers every day for the story of the murder of Amos Hurst. But no story appeared. Five days later he found Hurst's name in the obituary column. It said Amos Hurst had died accidentally. Mac-Donald couldn't believe his eyes. Until then, MacDonald had been in terror of the police arresting him for murder, even though he was certain that no-one had seen him leave Hurst's room.

Now he realised how easy it was to commit murder and get away with it, MacDonald bought a sheath-knife and went looking for someone to kill.

MacDonald met a man named 'Bill' in a wine saloon. The more they drank, the more Bill looked like the corporal who had raped him all those years before. At closing time, the pair took a couple of bottles of sherry to the nearby park for a drink. MacDonald's urge to kill was strong, but he waited until his drinking partner passed out drunk on the grass. Then, taking the knife from its sheath, he was just about to plunge the blade into Bill's neck when the urge left him. He sat on the man's chest with the knife raised, but the desire to commit murder had gone. He put the knife back in its sheath and went home, leaving the world's luckiest wino to sleep it off.

William MacDonald moved to Sydney in January 1961, where he found accommodation in East Sydney and took a job as a letter sorter with the PMG under the assumed name of Alan Edward Brennan. He became well known around the parks and public toilets that were the meeting places of homosexuals. For months he had no desire to kill anyone, but the urges to do so started creeping back.

On the night of Saturday, 4 June 1961, MacDonald struck up a conversation with a forty-five-year-old derelict, Alfred Reginald Greenfield, who was sitting on a bench in Green

Park, opposite St Vincent's Hospital in the inner-city Sydney suburb of Darlinghurst. MacDonald offered Greenfield a drink from his bottle and lured him to the nearby Domain Baths on the pretext that he had more bottles in his bag. MacDonald had bought a brand new knife for the occasion. The blade was about six inches long and razor sharp.

By day, the Domain Baths was a popular public swimming spot situated on Sydney Harbour. By night the Domain's environs were the haunt of derelicts. There were many alcoves to conceal the drinkers from the winter chill.

MacDonald and Greenfield chatted away as they shared another bottle of beer on the ten-minute walk to the Domain, where they settled into a secluded corner. The need to kill Alfred Greenfield had by now become overwhelming. But MacDonald controlled his urge until the man had drunk all of the beer and had gone to sleep on the grass.

William MacDonald removed the knife from its sheath as he knelt over the sleeping derelict. He brought it down swiftly and buried the blade deep into his victim's neck. He lifted and plunged the knife again and again until Alfred Greenfield lay still.

The ferocity of the attack had severed the arteries in Greenfield's neck. Blood was everywhere but the Mutilator had come prepared. He had brought a light plastic raincoat in his bag and had put it on before he attacked Greenfield.

The Mutilator removed his victim's trousers and underpants, lifted the testicles and penis and hacked them off at the scrotum with his knife.

The Mutilator then threw Alfred Greenfield's genitals into the harbour, wrapped his knife in his raincoat, put it in his bag and walked home. He stopped along the way and washed his hands and face under a tap. Nobody seemed to have noticed the Mutilator as he walked home on that showery, dark night. If they did, they didn't remember him.

There was no way that William MacDonald wouldn't read about this murder in the paper. The following day it was all over the front pages of the evening press. They called it the work of a maniac. They dubbed him 'the Mutilator'.

The press couldn't print the full extent of Alfred Greenfield's injuries, but the rumours spread like wildfire. They did say that he had been violently stabbed at least thirty times and certain parts of his anatomy were found floating in the harbour.

However, the police were at a loss to come up with the slightest motive why anyone would want to murder a derelict, let alone cut off his genitalia and leave them floating near the scene of the crime. They conducted an intense investigation, but found nothing. Not the slightest clue.

Within a couple of months, Sydney had

forgotten about the Mutilator. Police wound down their investigations and the savage murder of Alfred Greenfield became another unsolved crime. But when another derelict turned up dead six months later the similarities between the murders were unmistakable and police knew there was a serial killer on the loose.

In each case a drunken vagrant had been violently stabbed to death. And his penis and testicles had been sliced off. But this time the missing appendages were nowhere to be found.

On the morning of Saturday, 12 November 1961, William MacDonald purchased a knife with a six-inch blade from a Sydney sports store. He told the man behind the counter that he was going fishing. But he really wanted it to commit murder. The urges to kill were back, and they were stronger than ever.

That night, MacDonald was walking down South Dowling Street in East Sydney when he saw fifty-five-year-old Ernest William Cobbin staggering towards him.

MacDonald lured Cobbin to nearby Moore Park, where they sat in the public toilets and drank beer. Cobbin made no comment when his new friend put on a raincoat from his bag. Ernest Cobbin was sitting on the toilet seat when the first blow from the knife struck him in the throat, severing his jugular vein.

The Mutilator had brought the knife up in a sweeping motion, the same way that a fighter delivers an uppercut, and it had the desired effect. Ernest Cobbin's blood sprayed everywhere, all over the Mutilator's arms, face and raincoat. Cobbin instinctively lifted his arm to defend himself as the Mutilator kept stabbing, wounding Cobbin on the arms, neck, face and chest.

Even when Ernest Cobbin fell stone dead from the toilet seat, the Mutilator kept up the frenzied attack. There was blood all over the toilet cubicle. The Mutilator was revelling in it. He pulled Ernest Cobbin's pants and underpants down to his knees, lifted his penis and testicles, cut them off with his knife and put them in a plastic bag.

When he had finished, the Mutilator calmly took off his raincoat, wrapped his knife and the plastic bag in it, put them in his bag and walked out of the toilet. He stopped along the way to wash his hands under a tap.

Back at his lodgings, the Mutilator washed the bloody contents of the plastic bag in warm water, put them in a clean plastic bag and took them to bed with him.

The following day the Mutilator wrapped the plastic bag, the knife and a brick in newspaper, tied them with string and threw them from the Sydney Harbour Bridge. This time there would be no evidence left floating around. On the Monday morning, MacDonald went back to his job of sorting letters as if nothing had happened.

Meanwhile, the headlines in the newspapers read 'Mutilator Strikes Again'. The horror that the police had discovered was unimaginable. Ernest Cobbin had been stabbed about fifty times. There was blood everywhere. There was no doubt that if anyone had walked in on the Mutilator as he went about his business, he too would have been stabbed to death.

Again, the police couldn't find a clue. There were no fingerprints, not even on the beer bottle. The Mutilator had wiped it clean. No-one had seen a thing. Police staked out public toilets and known derelict haunts. Undercover police disguised as vagrants mixed with the down and outs of the many wine bars and hotels that catered for that type of clientele. It all proved fruitless.

As the months passed, police had to concede that they were no closer to catching the Mutilator than they were when Alfred Greenfield's body was discovered near the Domain Baths. But where and when would he strike again? They could only wait and see.

After the murder of Ernest Cobbin, William MacDonald's rage had subsided and he went about his life as usual. He read every newspaper story about his exploits, but had great difficulty in understanding that he was reading about himself. It was as if another person was doing these dreadful things and MacDonald was merely an onlooker. It frightened him.

He joined in with his workmates in

discussions about the mysterious Mutilator and listened to their theories of what type of person he may be. MacDonald would secretly get upset when they referred to the mystery murderer as a 'queer' and a sexual deviate. He knew differently.

For a time, MacDonald thought his work-mates suspected him of being the Mutilator, but it was only his own paranoia. The thought of giving himself up to police also crossed his mind, but he admitted to himself that he enjoyed the killing too much to do anything as silly as that.

As the months went by, the urge to kill again became overwhelming. On the morning of Saturday, 31 March 1962, William MacDonald purchased another long-bladed, razor-sharp sheath knife from Mick Simmons sports store in the Haymarket. He packed it in his bag with his raincoat and a plastic bag.

It was raining slightly that night and William MacDonald was wearing his raincoat. At 10 p.m. he left the Oxford Hotel in Darlinghurst and followed Frank Gladstone McLean down Bourke Street and past the Darlinghurst Police Station. MacDonald struck up a conversation with the drunken McLean and suggested that they turn into Bourke Lane and have a drink.

As they rounded the unlit corner, the Mutilator plunged the knife into McLean's throat. Frank McLean was a big man, well over six feet tall, and could have made mincemeat of the smaller MacDonald had he not been so drunk. McLean felt the knife sink deep into this throat and started to resist.

The Mutilator stabbed him again in the face and as McLean fell about, trying to protect himself, the Mutilator punched him in the face, forcing him off balance. As McLean fell to the ground, the Mutilator was on him. He stabbed McLean about the head, neck, throat, face and chest until he was dead.

Saturated in Frank McLean's blood, Mac-Donald dragged the body a few metres further into the lane, lowered his victim's trousers and, slicing the knife from the bottom in an upward stroke, cut off McLean's genitals.

This time the Mutilator was frightened that he would be caught in the act. He had committed the murder only a few yards from busy Bourke Street. As he put the genitals in his plastic bag, he feared that someone may see him. He had heard voices as people walked past the entrance to the laneway and in his paranoia he expected a police car to pull up any minute. But his luck held.

William MacDonald peeked around the laneway and, satisfied that no-one was coming, wrapped his knife and the plastic bag in the raincoat, put it in his bag and strolled down Bourke Street. He also took the bottle of sweet sherry that he and McLean had been drinking, as it was covered in fingerprints. He passed several people along Bourke Street, but they paid him no attention. For the third or fourth time now, the Mutilator had escaped as if he was invisible.

Back at his room, the Mutilator washed the contents of the plastic bag in the sink, then put them in a clean plastic bag. In the morning he threw the incriminating evidence off the Harbour Bridge.

The police were relentless in their hunt for the Mutilator. The murders were unprecedented in Australian history. Police could not recall more violent or sickening crimes. One theory was that the murderer was a deranged surgeon. The removal of Frank McLean's genitals had been done with a scalpel by someone with years of surgical experience, the experts said. Doctors found themselves under investigation.

Police even listened to clairvoyants. The most notorious witch of the time, Rosaleen Norton, claimed to be in touch with the Mutilator when she had her daily chats with the Devil. Police investigated, just in case.

A special police task force was set up to track down the killer who was causing them so much embarrassment. Teams of detectives worked around the clock checking out every possible lead. And there were plenty of possible leads. Police phones ran hot. Houses were raided on the slightest suspicion that the Mutilator might be hiding there. Night shelters and hostels were checked and rechecked. Nothing. Still the Mutilator eluded police.

But things were not going quite so well for William MacDonald in his private life. In totally unrelated incidents, he had a severe falling out with his landlord and in the same week he got the sack from the PMG.

MacDonald had saved a lot of money over the years and he decided to go into business for himself. Still using the assumed name of Alan Edward Brennan, he paid £560 for a mixed business in Burwood, an inner Western suburb of Sydney. In his little shop, William MacDonald made sandwiches and sold a variety of smallgoods. The shop was also an agency for a dry cleaning company. MacDonald lived in the residence above the business and for the first time in his life he was left alone. He loved it. He had no landlord standing over him and he didn't have to answer to anyone at work.

So when the urges to kill came on him again, the Mutilator didn't have to worry about the risk of being caught doing his thing in a public place. He could bring his victims home.

On Saturday night, 6 June 1962, William MacDonald went to a wine saloon called the Wine Palace, opposite the People's Palace in Pitt Street in the heart of downtown Sydney. Here he met forty-two-year-old James Hackett, a petty thief and derelict who had only been out of gaol for a couple of weeks.

They went back to MacDonald's new residence and continued drinking until Hackett passed out on the floor. MacDonald used a boning knife from his delicatessen to stab the sleeping Hackett. On the first plunge, the long knife went straight through Hackett's neck, but, incredibly, Hackett woke up and shielded the next blow with his arm. This diverted the knife into MacDonald's other hand, cutting it badly.

With blood pouring from the wound in his hand, the Mutilator unleashed renewed homicidal rage on Hackett. He brought the knife down with both hands and plunged it through Hackett's heart, killing him instantly. The floor was awash with blood. But still the Mutilator attacked Hackett's body with the knife until he had to stop for breath.

He sat in the pools of blood beside the body, puffing and panting. There was blood everywhere. It was splattered all over the walls and the ceiling; it had collected in big puddles on the floor.

The Mutilator bandaged his hand with a dirty dishcloth and set about removing Hackett's genitals. But the knife was now blunt. He had stabbed Hackett so many times that his bones had blunted the blade. Too tired to go down to the shop to get another one, the Mutilator sat covered from head to foot in blood, hacking away at Hackett's scrotum with the blunt knife. He stabbed the penis a few times and made some cuts around the testicles before finally giving up and falling asleep where he sat.

In the morning the Mutilator woke to find

himself covered in sticky, drying blood. He was lying next to the victim Hackett. The pools of blood had soaked through the floorboards and threatened to drip onto the counters of his shop.

William MacDonald had a bath, cleaned himself up and went to the hospital where he had some stitches put in his hand. He told the doctor that he had cut himself in his shop. It took MacDonald the best part of the day to clean up the mess. The huge pools of blood on the linoleum couldn't be scrubbed out and he had to tear it up, break it into bits and throw it out.

MacDonald dragged the dead Hackett underneath his shop and left him there. Every few hours he went back to the body and dragged it a little further into the foundations of the building until it was jammed into a remote corner of the brickwork, out of view and almost impossible to see. MacDonald left all of his bloodied clothing with the corpse.

When he finally sat down and thought about what he had done, MacDonald panicked. He thought that the police would come looking for Hackett. Few of the bloodstains had come off the walls and there was blood all over the floorboards. If the police even came to ask him questions, he would be caught. And then there was the cab driver who had driven them to the shop on the night of the murder. He would remember them.

On the Monday morning, William Mac-Donald packed his bags and caught a train to Brisbane, where he moved into a lodging house, dyed his greying hair black, grew a moustache and assumed the name of Alan MacDonald. Every day he bought the Sydney papers, expecting to read of the murder of Hackett and how police were looking for a man named Brennan in connection with the Mutilator murders.

But as the days turned into weeks and months, there was no mention of any body or any search for the missing Brennan. Mac-Donald was beside himself with worry. Had police found the body and set a trap for him? Would they knock on his door at any minute? The mystery of it all was driving him crazy.

However, although he didn't know it, the Mutilator didn't have a worry in the world. He had been declared dead, and no-one was looking for a dead man.

A few days after MacDonald left for Brisbane, customers wanting to pick up their dry cleaning had become concerned that no-one was at the shop. Neighbours assumed that the nice Mr Brennan had left without telling anyone.

After three weeks, a putrefying smell was coming from the vicinity of the empty shop. After a month the smell was so overwhelming that neighbours called the Health Department, who in turn called the police to break the door in. The smell in the shop was hideous. It led police to the rotting body of Hackett.

The corpse was so badly decomposed it was impossible to identify. The police bundled it into an ambulance and sent it off to the morgue at nearby Rydalmere Hospital. The body was so putrid that the mortician carried out the autopsy in a shed in the hospital grounds. The only thing they could determine was that it was a male aged about forty, the same age as the missing Brennan.

The body was taken and buried in a plot in the hospital grounds. At this stage police assumed it was the body of the missing shop proprietor, Alan Brennan, who had crawled under his shop for reasons known only to himself and electrocuted himself. Police had no reason to suspect foul play. Everything was normal. It looked like an accidental death.

When his workmates at the PMG read of the unfortunate demise of their old workmate in the death notices they attended the small memorial service conducted by a local funeral director. Alan Edward Brennan was laid to rest and police started looking for any next of kin. William MacDonald was a free man if only he had known it, and if he had never gone back to Sydney he may well have been a free man still.

MacDonald stayed a short time in Brisbane before going to New Zealand, still in the belief that the police would be looking for him. But the urge to kill was still with him and it was getting stronger every day. He had to kill again, and for some reason he had to return to Sydney to do so.

About six months after the 'death' of Alan Brennan, one of his old work-mates, John McCarthy, was walking down George Street in Sydney when he bumped head on into the 'dead' Brennan. McCarthy nearly died of shock himself.

As he had no idea that the murdered Hackett had been buried as the missing Brennan, Mac-Donald was surprised when his old work friend was so shocked to see him. The two men went and had a drink together.

'You're supposed to be dead,' McCarthy told MacDonald.

'What do you mean?' the puzzled Mac-Donald asked.

'They found your body underneath your shop at Burwood. We went to your funeral service,' McCarthy replied. 'But if you're alive, who was the body under your shop? And why did you run away?'

As it dawned on MacDonald what had happened, he jumped up and ran from the hotel. That night he was on a train to Melbourne.

John McCarthy went to the police, but they didn't believe him when he told them that he had just had a drink with a dead man. The desk sergeant told him to go home and sleep it off. And they didn't believe him the following day when he went back and told them the same story again. They said he was crazy.

In desperation John McCarthy rang the *Daily Mirror* and spoke to Joe Morris. 'I listened to the story before interviewing him. He didn't sound crazy to me,' recalled Joe. The *Mirror* ran the story and the legendary 'Case of the Walking Corpse' headline came about.

An embarrassed police commissioner was forced to exhume the corpse and from what was left of the fingerprints, they discovered that the body was that of the petty thief Hackett and not Brennan. Closer examination revealed the stab wounds and the mutilation to Hackett's penis and testicles. Police knew that at long last they were onto the Mutilator.

John McCarthy supplied an identikit of the missing MacDonald and it was circulated on the front page of every paper across the nation. MacDonald had taken a job on the railways in Melbourne and even though he had dyed his hair and had a light moustache, there was no mistaking that he was the missing Brennan MacDonald's new work-mates were onto him in a flash and as MacDonald asked the station master for his pay for the three days that he had worked, the police arrived and took him into custody.

William MacDonald confessed to everything. Charged with four counts of murder, he pleaded not guilty on the grounds of insanity. His trial, held in September 1963, was one of the most sensational the country had ever seen. The public hung onto every word of horror that fell from the Mutilator's mouth as he told of the murders and the bloodbath in great detail. As jurors fainted and women had to be carried from the public gallery, the trial of the Mutilator built to its sensational close.

The jury didn't take long to find William MacDonald guilty of four counts of murder. As everyone thought that the Mutilator was crazy, there was yet another sensation when the jury chose not to go with public opinion and found him to have been sane at the time of the murders.

Before passing sentence, Mr Justice McLennan said that it was the most barbaric case of murder and total disregard for human life that had come before him in his many years on the bench. William MacDonald had shown no signs of remorse and had made it quite clear that, if he were free, he would go on killing as often as the urges came upon him.

William ('the Mutilator') MacDonald was sentenced to prison for life with the strong recommendation that he never be released. He is currently in high security in Cessnock prison.

In prison, the Mutilator is known as Bill. He has been in prison for so long now that he is 'institutionalised'. So much has changed during his prison years that he could not survive for long on the outside.

But no-one's taking any chances. Staff a Cessnock prison say that the Mutilator' papers are marked: 'Likely to offend again'.

2 The Demon Inside Lenny

After he had sentenced Leonard Keith Lawson to death for the rape of two women in 1954, Mr Justice Clancy did an extraordinary thing. As Lawson was being led from the dock to go through the trapdoor into the cells below, the elderly judge summoned him back and said:

'Before you leave, I want to add this. It is not my practice, where a sentence is fixed by parliament, to make any observations. In your case I propose to depart from that practice.

'I should not want you to leave this court in the belief that you can expect any clemency in any recommendation by me. I accept the law as it is, and I think it is a proper law, and a just law. I think that in your case there is no reason why it should not be carried into execution.'

The gallery erupted in applause at the judge's comments. Lenny Lawson's crime had shocked the nation. However, Justice Clancy's words were in vain. Not only would Lawson beat the death penalty, he would live to be released from prison to add murder to his list of crimes.

There was nothing obvious in Lenny Lawson's upbringing to suggest his future crimes. From a loving, middle-class country family, he and his younger sister both enjoyed good educations at the Wagga High School. Here, Lenny gained the Intermediate Certificate and was top of his class.

The popular, good-looking young Lawson left school at age fifteen and went to work for a publishing firm in Sydney as an apprentice commercial artist. Out of his time at seventeen, he started freelancing, mainly with the same firm, and his work was good enough for him to make a comfortable living. Lawson was the illustrator of the popular *Lone Avenger* and *Hooded Rider* comic-book characters. But Lawson had a secret. He was also making money by selling his pornographic drawings. Lawson's obsession was naked women and sex and his obscene drawings were extremely graphic. Not only that, but in some of them the girls appeared to be dead.

Lawson married his childhood sweetheart at nineteen; the marriage produced two sons and a daughter, and life was looking good. As well as his drawing work, Lenny set up a photographic studio and specialised in photographing beautiful young models.

On 7 May 1954, twenty-six-year-old Lenny Lawson took five young models on an assignment into the bushes at Terrey Hills on the outskirts of Sydney. The girls would later say that they felt at ease with Lenny, as some of them had posed for him before. They found him to be a 'fun guy'. And some didn't mind having sexy conversations with Lenny as he was a happily married man with a young family. They felt secure. Most were prepared to engage in a little harmless flirting with the good-looking young photographer with the Clark Gable moustache.

So when Lenny produced a sawn-off .22 rifle and a hunting knife instead of his camera, the girls thought it was a joke. But Lenny wasn't kidding and it took only a minute to convince the girls that he was deadly serious. Lawson's life revolved around sexual fantasies, but now they would become his reality. Today he would enact his favourite.

Lawson told police that in his fantasy he was an Arabian sheikh who had captured five beautiful young girls and was holding them against their will. The sheikh knew that the girls were secretly in love with him and would worship him forever as soon as he had made love to them all. They actually wanted to be tied up. They actually wanted sex with the dashing young sheikh. Then they would surrender themselves to him forever. Or so Lawson thought.

Lawson had come prepared. From his bag he produced lengths of rope that had been pre-cut to the right length to bind the girls. There were two pieces for each girl. One for the wrists and one for the ankles. Producing a big pair of scissors to cut off the girls' clothing, he caressed each girl as he cut off their garments and tied her up. When they were all naked he lined them up in front of him and gagged them with sticking plaster taken from his bag.

Lawson removed all of his clothes and paraded naked in front of the girls. Then he made four of the girls sit on rocks in a semicircle while he raped the youngest, a fifteen-year-old, in front of them. He then sat back on a rock and forced a twenty-two-year-old married woman, in full view of the others, to have sex with him. Eventually Lawson untied his victims. He then told them that he had done a 'terrible thing' and that he was going into the bush to kill himself. Although they were still terrified, the girls pleaded with Lenny to think of his wife and children. They promised that if he drove them back to the city they wouldn't tell anyone about the rapes.

Lenny believed that his fantasy had become a reality. Even though he hadn't taken any photos, Lenny still paid the girls their assignment fees for the day. On the way back to Sydney, one of the girls asked to stop at a shop for cigarettes. There, she rang the police.

They were waiting for Lenny when he arrived back at his studio.

Offering no resistance when he was arrested, Lenny Lawson seemed surprised that he was charged with rape and indecent assault. He claimed that the girls were willing partners.

The tabloid press had a ball with Lenny, going as far as they possibly could in those conservative times. Every scrap of information about the case was sensationalised and an outraged public called for Lawson's blood. He was labeled 'The Terror of Terrey Hills' and 'The Beast of the Bushland'. The laws of the time were particularly harsh on rapists, and as Lenny's crimes were unprecedented, almost everyone wanted the maximum penalty for Lawson — death by hanging.

Lawson's trial began on 24 June 1954. From the first day the gallery was packed with women who had come to look at the handsome young man who claimed that five women had lured him into the bush, forced him to undress and tie them up and then have sex with them. Lawson pleaded not guilty but offered little defence, simply maintaining in his statement that the girls were all willing parties to the attacks. His defence counsel, Mr Jack Thom, had little to work with. All he could offer in his closing address for the defence was that: 'The facts did not establish a case of rape, but a "burlesque on the theme of rape", in which everyone took part willingly'.

The Crown prosecutor, Mr L. C. Furnell, in his closing address, said: 'The story of the accused is that, far from being the "Beast of the Bushland", he was the "Babe in the Wood", taken there by these scheming females to satisfy their lascivious tastes, and to give them the thrill of being raped. That is what you have to accept if you come to this conclusion that these girls are deliberately committing perjury to put a noose around this man's neck.'

Mr Furnell claimed that Lawson had deliberately and callously laid a plan, prepared the means, followed the course, and carried it to its final execution. He added: 'If you don't believe the stories of the girls, can you throw overboard the seven written confessions he made to the police? The statements match entirely the stories told by the girls.'

The court also heard the report of consulting psychiatrist, Dr John McGeorge:

'He [Lenny Lawson] is a very unstable individual and probably belongs to the psychopath class, that is he is not in any sense insane but could develop further and become more obviously abnormal. He appears to be lacking in moral sense and takes an almost morbid pride in the offence with which he has been charged. He is prepared to discuss it at considerable length and in complete detail. His account corresponds quite closely with that given in evidence by various witnesses. He is not insane. He is fit to plead.'

Lawson's father and the five models involved in the case were in the court when he was found guilty of double rape. Lawson bowed his head, but showed no emotion when the jury returned its verdict after a two-hour deliberation.

Asked whether he had anything to say before sentence was passed on him, Lawson shook his head. Mr Justice Clancy then pronounced the death sentence. The citizens of Australia prayed this would be the last anyone would hear of Leonard Keith Lawson. But this was not to be the case.

A month after the sentencing, Dr McGeorge interviewed Lawson again and wrote this report:

'This extraordinary young man is quite cheerful and contented with his lot. There is no doubt that he is extremely unstable and an exhibitionist in the true sense of the term. The whole episode was probably planned with a view to publicity. His original intention was to commit suicide after the incident but like all his type he lacked the courage to do it.

'The only thing that has shaken his complacency was the surprising comment of the judge after sentence. Obviously until then he had regarded it as an exciting, even an interesting experience. He is a psychopath but it is doubtful that he will ever be certified. Although he knows that he must serve a long sentence he is already making plans for his employment on his release. His judgment and moral sense are sadly defective.

'He is not insane by any means and has quite a good measure of intelligence. He will probably turn his sentence to a good profit and will be a model prisoner and thus a sore trial to those with whom he associates.'

While the death sentence passed on Lenny Lawson sparked widespread controversy among social groups and politicians, Lawson did nothing about an appeal. He chose to do his paintings and drawings in the comfort of his cell at Long Bay gaol while he allowed the New South Wales Labor government to lodge an appeal for him. As a result, his death sentence was commuted to fourteen years in prison.

True to the psychiatrist's words, Lenny was a model prisoner who studied portrait painting and taught other prisoners drawing skills. His specialty was painting famous people and at one stage it was suggested that Lenny's work should be considered for the Archibald Prize. When it was discovered that the portrait must be painted from a live model and not a photograph, the project was abandoned.

Lenny gave over to God in his prison years and said he found great strength in embracing the Catholic faith. He painted scenes from the Bible on the walls of the Goulburn prison chapel. Clergy came from all over the country to marvel at the work of the reformed man. God had worked a miracle on Lenny Lawson.

When he came up for parole in late 1960,

Lawson was at a low-security prison farm in southern New South Wales. As far as his supporters were concerned, Lenny had paid his debt to society. He would be an asset to the community. The letters to the Parole Board recommending his release used such words as 'exemplary', 'reformed' and 'miraculous'.

The day after Lord Fury won the 1961 Melbourne Cup, Lenny Lawson was back on the front pages of the newspapers. And the allegations against him this time relegated the usually huge Cup stories to a minor item. Lenny had been charged with murdering two young women. The headline in the *Sydney Morning Herald* read: 'Artist on Two Charges of Murdering Girls'. The article went on to report: 'Leonard Keith Lawson, 34, artist of Anzac Ave., Collaroy, was charged in Moss Vale Court last night with the murder of two girls. Police alleged that Lawson stabbed a girl at Collaroy on Monday night after attempting to strangle her and shot another girl dead at Moss Vale yesterday.'

Due to the rules of *sub judice*, the press was not allowed to mention that Lawson had just been released from prison after serving only seven years of a death sentence for multiple rape. Information about a charged person's past had to be suppressed as it could be considered to have an influence on the jury.

But to a bewildered general public it sounded all too familiar. Was this the same Lenny

Lawson who should have been executed or locked away forever only a few years earlier? If so, what was he doing on the loose? No one could publicly ask these questions until after the trial, but public outrage continued to grow.

The Minister of Justice, Mr N. J. Mannix, confirmed that Lawson had been released from gaol on 27 May 1961. Mr Mannix told State Parliament on 8 November 1961 (the day after the murder of the two girls), that a parole board was set up in 1950 to examine the cases of individual prisoners recommended for release. The Board consisted of Judge A. S. Lloyd, a former District Court judge (chairman); Dr J. A. McGeorge, consulting psychiatrist to the Attorney-General's Department; Mr L. J. Nott, former controller-general of prisons; and Mr J. V. Ramus, former superintendent of police.

In 1960, the parole board recommended Lawson's release. Before the recommendation, Lawson was given a psychiatric examination to which all sex offenders were subjected, which he passed with flying colours. A Prisons Department spokesman said that Lawson was released on parole only a few months before he would have been released with normal re-missions for good conduct. But by being released a few months earlier, Lawson was placed under parole conditions for the remainder of his fourteen-year sentence instead of being completely free.

This was of little consolation to the families of the dead girls, Jane Mary Bower and Wendy Sue Luscombe ... or the murdered girls themselves.

After his release from prison in May 1961, Lawson went to live with his parents in Moss Vale and bought a car with money borrowed from his mother. His wife had left him while he was in gaol and he made no attempt to see his children. Lawson later told psychiatrists: 'I did not make an effort to see the kids because I felt it was better for them if I do not see them, although I wished very much to be able to visit them'.

Just three months before the murders, Lawson moved to Sydney, where he found work as a commercial artist and moved into an apartment in the fashionable suburb of Collaroy on Sydney's lower north shore.

Lenny Lawson's trial was heard before Justice McClements in front of a packed gallery at the Central Criminal Court on 16 July 1962. During the trial, Lawson, wearing dark horn-rimmed glasses and a blue suit, sat placidly in the dock, occasionally fingering his moustache.

When the trial began, Lawson stood in the dock, his hands clasped in front of him, and in an almost inaudible voice pleaded not guilty to the charge of murdering Jane Mary Bower at Collaroy on 6 November 1961.

Sergeant George Westerberg, of Collaroy,

then told how Miss Bower's body was found. There were two single beds in Lawson's Collaroy flat. On one was a pile of male clothing and on the other was the body of Miss Bower, clad only in red briefs. There were bruises high on the left side of her forehead, weals around her neck and wrists and a deep one-inch chest wound. Written on the front of her body, apparently with black crayon, were the words, 'God forgive me, Len'.

Detective Senior Constable Colin Leatherbarrow of the Scientific Bureau gave evidence of examining the body and the flat on 7 November. Later that day at Bowral Police Station, about 200 kilometres south of Sydney, he saw Lawson with other police, including Detective Sergeant Bateman. Bateman handed him a letter dated 7 November which read in part:

'Dear Mum and Dad. I have done a shocking and dreadful thing. Whatever this monster that moves into my body is, it did it with vengeance this time. It was something entirely beyond my control — but it's so fantastic it must be hard to understand. But whatever it is, it sends sanity out of the window and then just as quickly after it is over, I come back to hard logic sanity which is a dreadful experience. I can't express the horror I feel at what I've done. Jane was one of the finest, sweetest and most virtuous girls I have known. As I am completely sane and rational now and I know I have to kill myself, for as long as I live I will only bring misery and unhappiness to all associated with me.'

The letter was signed, 'Your broken hearted son, Len'.

After he had raped and murdered Jane Bower, Lawson drove his car to Moss Vale, where his parents lived, about 200 kilometres south of Sydney. The court was told that Lawson had slept in the car overnight. Lawson turned up at the chapel at the Sydney Church of England Girls' Grammar School (SCEGGS) at Moss Vale at 9 a.m.

As the students and teachers arrived for morning prayers, Lawson held them at rifle point. As he had done at Terrey Hills in 1954, Lenny had come prepared. In his bag he had pieces of rope to tie the girls' hands. He told them that he intended to hold them hostage so that he could prolong his freedom and negotiate with the police. He warned them that he had killed once already and he had nothing to lose.

School headmistress, Miss Jean Turnbull, approached Lawson who menaced her with the rifle. At that stage police arrived in response to a phone call from one of the teachers. As Lawson turned to look at them, Miss Turnbull grasped the barrel of the rifle and attempted to wrest it from him. In the struggle, the rifle discharged five times and one of the shots struck and killed fifteen-year-old

Wendy Luscombe. Miss Turnbull suffered gunshot wounds to her hands before police overpowered Lawson.

The senior Crown prosecutor Mr W. J. Knight, QC, read to the court Lawson's statement about the death of Jane Bower:

'I first met Jane Bower about five weeks ago. She was one of the nicest kids you would ever meet in your life. I became friendly with her mother first and then I got to know Jane better. I went out with her and her mother a few times. As the time went by I became more and more physically attracted to Jane. I eventually got into a state of mind where I just had to have her. I made up my mind yesterday that I was going to have intercourse with her that night, whether she consented or not. I filled up one of my socks with sand from the beach to use on her if I had to. Then I cut up some lengths of rope in case I needed them and I went over to where Jane was working to pick her up.

'That would be about five o'clock. She works at the Empire Art Company in William Street in the city. Then we went down to DJ's and picked up her mother and then all went over to their place in Stewart Street, Manly. We had tea together there and then Jane came with me to my place. I was painting a portrait of Jane and I told her mother that I was going to do some more work on it. We got to my flat around eight o'clock, perhaps a bit before.

We just sat and talked and I tried to make advances to her and she tried to talk me out of it. At that stage I went and got the sock and hit her on the head with it. She was sitting on the lounge with her back towards me when I came out of the bedroom and hit her.

'Then I tied her hands and feet with the lengths of rope I had. Then when I saw she was unconscious I untied her feet. I slipped her shirt back off and took her bra off and then her suspenders and stockings and so forth and then I had intercourse with her. When I had finished I could see that she was starting to regain consciousness and I came to my senses then and realised what I had done. I could see that my freedom was slipping away and I thought that the only thing I could do was to kill her.'

'I got a piece of rope and put it around her neck and held it tight. She started to struggle and was half dead and half alive and I could not stand her suffering any more so I got a hunting knife and drove it into her chest. She stopped suffering then.

'After I had put the knife into her I carried her in and put her on the bed and put her pants back on. That is the hardest thing that I have ever had to do in my life. I had to clean up. Then I cleaned the knife and wrote the inscription on her with an eyebrow pencil. I wrote across her stomach "God forgive me, Len".

'I then put some stuff in a bag, turned out the lights, got into my car and drove away. I stopped at a phone box in Collaroy and rang Jane's mother and told her that Jane was ill, that I had arranged for a neighbour to look after her while I was away and that I would come down to Manly, pick her up and bring her back to my flat to look after Jane. I only wish now that I could turn back time. I have killed the girl I loved more than anything else in the world.'

Although the evidence and his confession would put Lenny behind bars forever, police weren't convinced that he had told the story the way it really happened. Forensic evidence indicated that Lawson thought the girl was dead when he was raping her and that when she came to he took the huge hunting knife and plunged it through her heart. Satisfied that she was now dead, he finished his ghastly deed. Police were certain that Lenny had performed an act of necrophilia, but it was too difficult to prove and would be too much for the dead girl's distraught family to cope with. They let it be. They had their man.

Lenny Lawson's only defence witness was the psychiatrist, Dr Oscar Schmalzbach, who said that in his opinion Lawson was sane at the time of the murder. He spoke of Lenny's sexual fantasies and of the 'demon' that Lawson claimed lived inside him.

Dr Schmalzbach said: 'I feel that the accused

knew the nature and the quality of his act and knew that what he was doing was wrong. Psychiatrically, his condition is one of a personality disorder in the form of an obsessive compulsive personality, with tendencies to rituals.'

In the afternoon, counsel for the defence, Mr D. Stewart, announced that Lawson would make a statement from the dock. In a clear soft voice, Lawson said:

'Your Honour, gentlemen, you have heard the evidence for the prosecution and I admit that, in the main, it is true. I cannot explain what made me do this terrible thing because I don't know. It was something beyond my control. But I do know that since that night I have suffered remorse to a degree that words cannot express. No matter what the final verdict of this court is, for the rest of my life, my great punishment will come at the hands of my own conscience. I realise that remorse alone cannot make amends — no human agency can forgive me for what I did. So I can do nothing but simply throw myself on the mercy of this court.'

At 3.21 p.m. the jury retired to consider its verdict and at 3.38, just seventeen minutes later, they returned with a verdict of guilty. Mr Justice McClemens sentenced Lawson to 'the one sentence provided by the law for murder' — life imprisonment. From the disappointment in his voice, it was clear that he would much rather have seen Lawson at the end of a rope.

Lenny Lawson was back in the headlines on 19 June 1972 when he pleaded guilty to maliciously wounding Sharon Margaret Hamilton, a member of a concert group which visited Parramatta gaol on 18 June.

Detective Sergeant R. Shackleton told the court that after the concert, the sixteen professional musicians had been offered light refreshments by an arts and crafts group at the gaol. Lawson was secretary of the group.

After thanking the artists, Lawson, who had been standing behind Miss Hamilton, placed his left arm around her chest and held a knife near her throat. He then ordered everyone out of the room. In a struggle between Lawson and a number of inmates to free Miss Hamilton, she received a number of cuts requiring stitches.

In sentencing Lawson to a further five years on top of his existing life sentence, Judge Head said it was 'an empty but necessary formality'.

On 5 October 1979 the New South Wales Parole Board heard an application for the release of Leonard Keith Lawson. In rejecting the application, the board noted that 'drawings found in Lawson's flat showed clearly that deep seated in his warped mind were such matters as rape of schoolgirls, doctors' patients, artists' models and even female corpses'.

The Board also made special mention of the

notation made on Lawson's file in 1962 by the then minister for justice, Mr Mannix: 'While appreciating that I cannot bind the hand of any future Executive Government, I am strongly of the view that Leonard Keith Lawson should never be released'.

Lenny Lawson is in maximum security in Grafton prison.

3 The Voices from the Grave

On the fourth morning of his committal hearing for multiple murder, Archie McCafferty asked the judge if he could make a statement. Although it was an unusual request, the judge allowed it.

McCafferty said: 'Excuse me your worship, before the court starts, for the last four days I've sat here and listened to Mr Bannon criticising me on things that I've done. Now I've been wanting to say this for a long time, and I'm going to say it this morning. Mr Bannon, if you're listening, I'd like to cut your head off.'

It was not so much what McCafferty said that put a chill through the courtroom. It was the cold, methodical way in which he said it. McCafferty had already murdered three innocent people. The voice from the grave of his dead infant son had told him to kill seven. Then his boy would come back to him. Archie

McCafferty had four to go, and the decapitation of Mr Bannon would put him one closer to his target.

The Mr Bannon in question was a barrister acting for one of McCafferty's five co-accused. He proceeded with his case, safe in the knowledge that McCafferty was handcuffed and heavily guarded as he glared down from the dock. Archie McCafferty was also heavily drugged. Before the start of the committal hearings each morning, and throughout his following trial at the Central Criminal Court, he was given a heavy dose of tranquillisers to subdue his uncontrollable outbreaks of violence. The dosage was enough to bring a racehorse to its knees, yet in Archie's drug-soaked system it barely pacified him.

But the drugs did have some of the desired effects. During the twelve-day trial, Archie McCafferty had been alert and attentive. He listened closely to the evidence and made notes. He certainly didn't look like the deranged murderer who had been labelled 'Australia's Charles Manson'.

In fact McCafferty often winked at the court reporters and joked with his co-accused. He fingered the bench in the dock as though it were a keyboard and played tunes for the gallery. When the proceedings became tiresome, he deep-etched his name in the bench with a pen. Archie was having a ball. But without his medicinal straitjacket, the twenty-five-year-old Scotsman was a violent man who could kill without question.

While awaiting trial in Long Bay's remand section, Archie had nearly killed another prisoner with his slops bucket. The only way to calm Archie down was with sedatives. At first, normal doses had no effect. So prison doctors kept increasing the dosage until they took effect. His daily dosage of 1500 milligrams of the potent tranquilliser Largactil was almost four times the normal dose of 400 milligrams. Prison psychiatrists agreed that McCafferty's incredible tolerance to massive doses of tranquillisers was in itself evidence that he was insane. They also agreed that he should never be released from custody. There was no doubt in their minds that Archie would kill again.

Contrary to professional opinion, the jury found Archie to have been sane at the time of the killings. By rejecting his insanity plea they found him guilty of the senseless and cold-blooded murders of three men who just happened to be unlucky enough to fall into his hands as he went on a killing spree to avenge the accidental death of his six-week-old son.

Nobody shed a tear for the remorseless killer as the judge handed down the three life sentences. As he was led back to prison, McCafferty swore he would kill again. And there was no doubt in anyone's mind that, if he was given the chance, he would.

In the months leading up to the killings

Archie gave plenty of warning signs that he would turn into a killer. Concerned about his uncontrollable fits of rage, Archie checked himself into psychiatric hospitals on three occasions in the nine months.

In June 1972, he spent ten days at the Ryde Psychiatric Centre when his urges to hurt someone became too strong. Two months later, he admitted himself into the Parramatta Psychiatric Centre, where he complained of having murderous thoughts that were becoming too realistic. He was diagnosed as having an 'anti-social personality disorder'. Given Archie's explosive temper, he was like a stick of dynamite with a short fuse.

On top of this, Archie was taking any drugs he could get his hands on and mixing them with huge amounts of alcohol. Heroin, LSD, speed, marijuana, uppers, downers and the mind-altering hallucinogenic, angel dust, were all part of Archie's drug cocktail. Something had to give. And it did.

By March 1973, after the death of his son, the urges to kill his wife, her mother and her mother's boyfriend were so strong that Archie admitted himself again to the Parramatta Psychiatric Centre. In fact, the night before he admitted himself, Archie had tried to kill his wife.

Doctors diagnosed his problem as 'getting worse' but Archie was allowed to discharge himself. When asked at his trial how Archie

was allowed to walk out of hospital in such
a deranged state, a hospital spokesman
explained that they had no powers to hold
him. They knew that Archie McCafferty's body
clock was counting down to a monumental
explosion, but the only thing that they could
legally do was warn the police that there was
a potential madman on the loose.

This they did, alerting Blacktown police that
McCafferty was being released. The police
alerted Archie's family. After all, McCafferty
had gone to the hospital for help and openly
admitted that he was about to kill someone.
It was obvious that he desperately needed help
and if no-one could force him to stay and have
it, then the next best thing was to warn his
most likely victims.

His parents, Archie and Clementine, knew
that their son was deeply disturbed. When they
visited him in the psychiatric centre they were
told that his behaviour was a minor reaction
and that psychiatrists expected a much
stronger one in the near future. The 'minor
reaction' they were referring to was the attempt
by Archie to strangle his wife. His parents were
left wondering what the psychiatrists thought
the 'stronger reaction' might be. Sadly it would
be the deaths of three people Archie didn't
even know.

Archibald Beattie McCafferty had been in
trouble since he was old enough to walk. His
mother said he was a loving child with a quick

temper. When little Archie was ten his parents migrated to Australia from Scotland to leave behind their bleak working-class existence and start a new life with new hope. The McCaffertys moved first to Melbourne and then to Bass Hill in Sydney's west.

Archie was in trouble with the police from the outset and by the time he was twelve and placed in an institution for stealing, he already had a long record. By the time he was eighteen, Archie had been in institutions five times and had been classed as an incorrigible juvenile delinquent. One detective described him as 'the toughest kid I have ever met'. At twenty-four he had been in and out of gaol many times and had a record of thirty-five convictions that included break, enter and steal, stealing cars, larceny, assault, vagrancy and receiving stolen goods.

However, Archie McCafferty was not considered a violent criminal. His assault charges arose from fist fights with the police, but none of his other crimes involved violence. Yet Archie was obsessed with ferocity. He loved movies that overdosed on aggression and brutality. His favourites were *A Clockwork Orange* and *The Godfather*. He saw them many times over and his favourite scene from *The Godfather* was the one in which Sonny Corleone was riddled with bullets at the toll gates. Though at this stage in his life, Archie was not violent toward other people, he told a psychiatrist that he enjoyed strangling chickens, dogs and cats to see what it was like.

When Archie married Janice Redington in April 1972, his family prayed that he would at last settle down. The couple had met at a hotel where Janice worked part-time as a switchboard operator. The marriage was only six weeks old when Janice caught her husband in bed with another woman. She wasn't impressed, but Archie's response was so violent it prompted his first visit to a psychiatric hospital.

After discharging himself, Archie threw away his sedatives, started drinking heavily and took out all of his aggression on his wife. Although Janice was pregnant, Archie would repeatedly bash her when he was drunk, which was most nights. He would press his thumbs against her windpipe and only let go as she was about to lapse into unconsciousness.

One night when he nearly killed Janice, Archie booked himself back into the hospital. This was when he told psychiatrists that he wanted to kill his wife and her family. He said he wanted to get the evil thoughts out of his head, but discharged himself a few days later. There was nothing that the doctors could do to keep him there.

The visits to psychiatric hospitals did nothing to change Archie's ways. He was straight back on the drink when he discharged himself and his drug intake increased. So did his fits of uncontrollable violence. He got a job on a garbage truck and this seemed to pacify him for a short time during the days. But at night he was getting worse.

Archie's mother claimed that the birth of his son, Craig Archibald, on 4 February 1973 turned Archie into a different person. Janice McCafferty did not agree. She said that he was still drinking heavily and taking all sorts of drugs. She was terrified to take the baby in the car for fear that Archie would have an accident and kill them all.

Little Craig lived only six weeks.

At 3.30 a.m. on the morning of Saturday, 17 March, Janice took the baby to bed with them to feed him. She dozed off and awoke at 9 a.m. As she told the inquest into the baby's death: 'I felt something underneath me in the bed. I jumped straight out of bed and I saw the baby's face and realised something was terribly wrong. There was blood on his face and on my nightie. My bra was still undone. I must have rolled over to my left and rolled onto my baby.'

At the inquest, held on 24 August 1973, the coroner, Mr John Dunn, said that the child had died accidentally when his mother went to sleep on top of him while breast-feeding. He completely exonerated Janice McCafferty and said: 'I must say in the interests of the welfare of the young mother, I cannot find anything to be critical of her for what happened.'

Archie McCafferty did not agree. He had left Janice a week after the tragedy, and although he did not attend the inquest into his son's death, he sent a scathing letter to the coroner, accusing Janice of murdering their son.

Was the death of his son all that Archie McCafferty needed to tip him over the edge? It was a question on which psychiatrists would sharply disagree. Certainly, the horror of his son's death played constantly on Archie's already troubled mind. But was it the match that had lit the fuse to the keg of dynamite that was about to explode?

The first eruption occurred a week after Craig's death. The McCaffertys had a few friends over for drinks after the funeral and when most of them had gone, Archie started playing a record called 'Nobody's Child' in remembrance of his dead son. An argument started and Janice McCafferty fled. Archie caught up with her hours later in Blacktown, where he accused her of killing his son. When Archie took to her with a fence picket, Janice's brother and another man stepped in and gave him a hiding.

The following day he turned up at his parents' house at Bass Hill. Badly bruised and covered in blood, he pleaded with his mother for help. She despaired at her confused son's plight and begged him to readmit himself to the hospital. That day, a family friend drove

Archie to the Parramatta Psychiatric Centre, where he booked in for treatment. It was his third self-admission in nine months, the one that prompted hospital staff to ring the police when he checked himself out a few days later.

Archie's passion was tattoos. Visiting the tattooist was like seeing his therapist. The tattooist knew all of Archie's innermost secrets. Archie confided in him, sought his advice and admired his opinions. As a result of the long hours Archie had spent having pictures put on his body, there wasn't much room left. He was covered in more than 200 of them. When police had to photograph all of Archie's 'identifying marks', they used many rolls of film.

There were even stars tattooed on his ear lobes. Like many of the others on his body, they were done with Indian ink and sewing needles while filling in the long hours in prison. Archie hated these 'nick' tattoos and whenever he was out of prison, he got them covered with 'proper' ones.

His body is a walking advertisement of his hatred of the police. One tattoo spread across his shoulders and back says: 'The man who puts another man under lock and key is not born of woman's womb'. Another says 'Kill and hate cops'. Archie has drawings of two bulldogs on his chest and two sharks on each shoulder. There are eyes tattooed on each of his buttocks and the bottom half of his body is covered in drawings depicting love and sex.

Archie had saved a space on his chest for a special tattoo. Until his son was killed, he didn't know what that tattoo would be. The day he discharged himself from the Parramatta Psychiatric Centre he went to the tattooist and had a memorial to his son etched on that special spot on his chest. It is of a cross-shaped tombstone embedded in a blood-red rose. It is inscribed: 'In Memory of Craig'.

Several weeks later, Archie paid another visit to his tattooist for another special tattoo. This time he would have his favourite number, 7, tattooed on the web between the thumb and forefinger. It was one of the few places left on Archie's body that was not already covered with ink. He had the number tattooed next to the head of a snarling panther.

Archie chose that number for two reasons. He had decided that seven people must die to avenge his son's death. Plus it was his lucky number. Curiously, the number seven would recur during McCafferty's rampage of murder. Archie McCafferty's first victim, George Anson, would be stabbed seven times. The second victim, Ronald Neil Cox, was the father of seven children. In reference to his family, Cox uttered the word 'seven' a few seconds before McCafferty shot him in the head. He never stood a chance.

Psychiatrists said that once the unfortunate Cox had said that word, he was a dead man. To the deranged McCafferty, the number seven had supernatural significance.

Janice McCafferty had not seen her husband in the five months since she visited him at the Psychiatric Centre the day after he had tried to kill her. But on 23 August 1973, the night before the inquest into little Craig's death, two bricks with notes wrapped around them were tossed through the window of her home in Blacktown.

The first note read: 'You and the rest of your family can go and get fucked because anyone who has anything to do with me is going to die of a bad death. You know who this letter is from so take warning because Bill is the next cab off the rank. Then you go one by one.' It was signed, 'you know who'. 'Bill' was Bill Riean, Janice McCafferty's mother's boyfriend.

The second note read: 'The only thing in my mind is to kill you, your mother and Bill Riean. This is not a bluff because I'm that dirty on all of you for the death of my son, but I can't let it go at that. I have a matter of a few guns so I'm going to use them on you all for satisfaction. Beware.'

The following night, 24 August, the killing started. McCafferty had chosen the day carefully. It was the first day of the inquest into the death of his son.

A week earlier, Archie McCafferty had formed a gang out of an odd assortment of teenagers and Carol Ellen Howes, a twenty-six-year-old woman he was living with. Archie met Howes and sixteen-year-old Julie Ann Todd when he was a patient at the Parramatta Psychiatric Centre. Carol Howes was the mother of three children aged from four to seven and was separated from her husband. In the previous two years, Carol had made three attempts on her own life by taking large doses of sleeping tablets.

Carol Howes told Archie that she intended to try to kill herself again and McCafferty talked her out of it. This formed a bond between the pair and before long they had moved into a flat in the inner western suburb of Earlwood. The teenager, Julie Todd, had met them both at the centre while she was being treated for mental disorders. McCafferty took her in with them when she had nowhere else to go.

McCafferty was living with Howes and Todd at the time of the murders. They were joined by Michael John (Mick) Meredith and Richard William (Dick) Whittington, two seventeen-year-olds McCafferty had met in a Bankstown tattooist's a few days earlier. Mick and Dick had a couple of rifles. The sixth member of the gang was seventeen-year-old Donald Richard (Rick) Webster, who McCafferty had met only days earlier through his brother.

Led by McCafferty, the gang chose their first victim. At just over five feet tall, fifty-year-old George Anson was an easy mark. He was a newspaper seller outside the Canterbury

Hotel and each evening after work he would drink at the hotel. Just after closing time on the evening of 24 August, Anson was spotted by the gang as he staggered down the street toward his home. They had been cruising the area in a stolen Volkswagen, looking for someone to beat up and rob. Archie was flying high on angel dust.

Anson offered no resistance. He was far too drunk. The gang dragged Anson into a side street. As McCafferty grabbed the older man around the throat, Anson called out: 'You young cunt'. They were the last words he would ever say. McCafferty went berserk and kicked Anson repeatedly in the head and ribs. Then Archie heard the voice for the first time. 'Kill seven. Kill seven. Kill, kill, kill...' George Anson was kneeling in the gutter when McCafferty produced the knife and plunged it into his back and neck seven times.

McCafferty gave the dying man one final kick in the face before running back to the car.

His young disciples were in awe of the blood-soaked McCafferty. All except Rick Webster.

'Why the fuck did you do that?' Webster asked.

'I stabbed him because he called me a young cunt. Now drive, you fucking idiot,' McCafferty screamed at the terrified teenager.

From that instant on McCafferty did not trust Rick Webster. He would have to die. That decision would be Archie's undoing.

Archie threw the blood-soaked knife to Julie, who hid it under the seat. So strong was Archie's spell over his gang that not another word was spoken about the killing of George Anson until they got back to the flat.

On the way the gang went to Hartee's drive-in fast-food bar where they ordered hamburgers while McCafferty cleaned up in the men's room. Archie was in the horrors. His son was talking to him from the toilet mirror and beckoning him to go with him. Archie reached out to touch him, but he was gone. 'Kill seven, kill seven...'

Back at the flat, Julie washed the blood from the murder weapon and returned it to McCafferty. Only then did he talk about the murder. 'I couldn't help myself,' he told them. 'I couldn't stop. I can't understand why I did it. A voice... it was Craig's voice... told me to kill, kill, kill.'

Three nights later, on 27 August, Archie took his gang to the Leppington cemetery to show them the grave of his son. Archie had been there many times with Carol Howe since the funeral. Howe said that they would sit at the grave and Archie would sob and say things like: 'The poor little bloke. He never stood a chance. It's not fair. It's not bloody fair.' On one occasion he had promised his son that he would avenge his death.

It was a cold, bleak night and the rain came down in sheets. Small patches of fog gave the cemetery an eerier atmosphere than usual. Archie was off his face on angel dust again. Now the voice was coming from the grave. It was telling him, 'Kill seven, kill seven, kill seven...'

Archie and his gang stayed at the grave for a while and then went to a nearby hotel, where they planned the night's events. All Archie wanted to do was get back to the grave... and the voice. He instructed his gang to take him back to the cemetery.

Along the way they dropped Julie Todd and Mick Meredith off to hitchhike. The plan was that as soon as a car stopped they would force the driver to the cemetery at gunpoint and the gang would rob him.

Back at the cemetery, Archie was spinning out. He could see a bright light over his son's grave. There was a figure standing just out of the light. Archie approached the person who said: 'Dad. Is that you Dad?' Archie knew that it was his son. He had come back from the grave.

'Is that you, Craig?' he asked.

'Yes Dad, it's me,' the voice replied.

'But son, it can't be. You're dead.'

'Do you want me to come back to you, Dad?'

'Of course I do. But how can you do that, son?'

'You've got to do something for me, Dad. Do this thing and I will come back to you. Do you want me to come back to you?'

'Yes. Yes. More than anything in the world. I will do anything to have you back. Anything. Anything you ask.'

'You must kill seven people. As soon as you do, you can have me back. But you must kill seven people. Kill seven. Kill seven. Kill seven...'

Moments later a car pulled into the cemetery and stopped about 150 metres from the graveside. In the car were Julie Todd and Mick Meredith. They were holding forty-two-year-old Ronald Neil Cox at gunpoint. A miner who had just finished his shift at the Oakdale colliery and was on his way home to Villawood in Sydney's western suburbs, Cox had felt sorry for the two kids hitchhiking in the rain and had stopped to give them a lift. It was a fatal mistake. Meredith had held a gun to his head and forced him to drive to the cemetery.

McCafferty left the graveside and ran over to them. Ronald Cox was forced to lie face down in the mud while McCafferty and Meredith held rifles at the back of his head. Cox begged for his life as the voices urged the murderous McCafferty on. 'Kill seven. Kill seven...' The number bounced around in Archie's twisted brain.

McCafferty turned to his gang and said. 'I'll have to knock him. He's seen all of our faces. Mick... kill him.'

'What are you saying Archie?'

'Fuck you. Kill him.'

Meredith and McCafferty then each shot Ronald Cox through the back of the head.

As they were leaving to drive to Liverpool, Archie looked over to his son's grave. The light was still shining over it and the shadowy figure was laughing loudly. Archie burst out laughing with his son. He later told detectives that his only regret about murdering Ronald Cox was that he wasn't closer to his son's grave so that some of Cox's blood could have dripped onto the plaque.

After the killing of Cox, the gang members returned to the McCafferty unit where they drank beer and watched TV.

But Archie could still hear the voices telling him to 'Kill seven' and he instructed two of his disciples to go and find him another victim. In the early hours of the following morning, twenty-four-year-old driving instructor, Evangelos Kollias, picked up Julie Todd and Dick Whittington as they hitchhiked along Enmore Road. Once in the car, Whittington produced a .22 rifle from under his coat. They forced Kollias into the back seat and told him to lie on the floor while Julie drove the car back to the flat.

McCafferty then took over. With Archie driving, the gang set off for Liverpool on the pretext of looking for a factory to rob. But they knew different. They knew that Archie had murder on his mind. Kollias was told to lie low as they did not want him to see where they were going. Assured that he would come to no harm, Kollias lay on the back floor and went to sleep.

Archie's plan was to kill Evangelos Kollias, then drive his car to Blacktown and kill Janice McCafferty, her mother and her mother's boyfriend. That would make six. The seventh victim was to be one of his own gang, Rick Webster. Archie felt that Webster was going to betray him to the police.

McCafferty told Whittington to kill Kollias. Whittington wasn't sure that he could, but as Kollias woke from his nap in the back of the car Whittington held the sawn-off .22 rifle to his head and pulled the trigger. Evangelos Kollias died instantly.

'Shoot him again,' urged McCafferty. Whittington put another bullet into the dead man's head. They dumped the body in a deserted street nearby.

When he realised that Kollias' car didn't have enough petrol to get him to his wife's house, Archie abandoned the plan to murder Janice and her family. For that night at least. He still intended to make them the next three victims. And if Rick Webster hadn't lived up to Archie's suspicions and gone to the police, there is no doubt that Archie would have killed them. The voice kept telling him to.

When detectives arrested him, Archie told them: 'I was going to Blacktown to kill three people... I was going to go into the house and just start blasting away until they were all dead. They are very lucky people that the car didn't have enough petrol.' He said he had intended to cut off his wife's head and send it in a box to the chief of the CIB.

When one of the gang members told Rick Webster that he was on Archie's hit list, Webster decided to tell what he knew to the police. McCafferty, Whittington and Meredith followed Webster to the *Sydney Morning Herald* building where he worked as an apprentice compositor. They sat in a stolen van out the front of the *Herald* building with loaded rifles, ready to kill Webster when he came out.

Webster saw them waiting and had a reporter call police. Detectives arrived at the *Herald*, where Webster told them he was too terrified to leave the building. When they heard his story about the three murders they called for reinforcements and the area was sealed off. Heavily armed detectives surrounded the vehicle while Detective Sergeant K. Aldridge approached it and pointed his revolver at Michael Meredith. Other detectives rushed the vehicle and apprehended McCafferty and Whittington. They took possession of two loaded and cocked rifles.

On the way to the police station, McCafferty told police: 'All right, I knocked the bloke at Canterbury. I knocked the bloke at Leppington. And I knocked the bloke at Merrylands. I knocked all three of them.' He made no less a secret of the fact that he would kill again.

At his sensational trial in February 1974, McCafferty pleaded not guilty to three counts of murder on the grounds of insanity. His five co-accused — Todd, Howe, Meredith, Whittington and Webster — all pleaded not guilty to the same charges.

The press had labelled the murders as 'thrill-killings' and everyone wanted to know about the Charles Manson like cult figure who had led his followers into an orgy of senseless killings. Archie didn't let the packed courthouse down. He told of the voice from the grave and how he had been told that seven must die if he wanted to see his son again. He maintained that he was completely insane at the time of the murders.

The press lapped it up, and Archie didn't disappoint them. At last he was getting the recognition that he so desperately craved. Even if he had to kill three people to get it. And in true trouper fashion, Archie saved the best bit until last, his statement which he read from the dock:

'Your Honour and gentlemen of the jury. Firstly, I would like to say that at the time of these crimes I was completely insane. The reason why I done this is for the revenge of my son's death. That is what made me do it.

'Before this I had stated to a doctor that I felt like killing people, but up until my son's death I had not killed anyone.

'My son's death was the biggest thing that

ever happened to me, because I loved him so much and he meant the world to me, and after his death I just seemed to go to the pack.

'I feel no wrong for what I have done, because at the time that I did it, I didn't think it was wrong. But after my son was killed, I tried to kill my wife then, and I was admitted into Parramatta Psychiatric Home because I knew I needed treatment. So I signed myself in, and I was there for a number of weeks.

'I think, if given the chance, I will kill again, for the simple reason that I have to kill seven people, and I have only killed three, which means I have four to go, and this is how I feel in my mind, and I just can't say that I am not going to kill anyone else, because in my mind I am.

'Whether you think I am sane or insane is up to youse [sic] but I would say that I was definitely insane at the night of these murders. The day of my son's inquest at the Coroner's Court happened to be the day that I stabbed Mr Anson. The reason why I killed this man was because I heard my son's voice tell me to do so. The same with the second and third person.

'Each time I went to the graveyard to visit my son's grave a violent streak would come over me, and I wanted to be so violent I wanted to kill people. I kept hearing voices, not only my son's voice, but other voices as well, which I don't know whose they are.

'On the Thursday that I was apprehended, I had every intention of killing Rick Webster, as I heard the voices to tell me to do so, and anyone else that the voices tell me to kill, I would kill until I reached the figure seven.

'I still say I felt no wrong in what I have done and I am still willing to kill anyone else that I am told to kill. At the time of my son's death, I took it pretty hard, and since then I have not been the same because I loved him so much, and I believe in my own mind that my wife murdered him on purpose, and that is why I killed these men, for the revenge of my son's death.

'And this is the honest truth. So I hope that the jury and Your Honour will believe what I said. That's it.'

At the trial, three psychiatrists gave their opinions of Archie's mental state. Dr William Metcalf, a Macquarie Street specialist, was called to give evidence on behalf of the defence. He said that in his opinion McCafferty was insane at the time of the killings because he did not know what he was doing was wrong. Dr Metcalf pointed out that Archie was mentally ill and his mind was not in tune with reality. He was a paranoid schizophrenic at the time of the killings.

A completely different opinion was given by the prosecution's psychiatric adviser, Dr Oscar Schmalzbach, also a Macquarie Street specialist and consultant psychiatrist to the state government. Dr Schmalzbach said: 'In my view, McCafferty knew at the time that what he was doing was wrong. He may have had an isolated schizophrenic reaction at the time of the second killing but this did not make him a paranoid schizophrenic. Such an illness does not exist one day and disappear another day and come back the third day.'

A third psychiatrist who examined McCafferty after the killings did not give evidence. He took the middle view that McCafferty was insane but he knew what he was doing at the time of the killings.

Although they could not agree on Archie's sanity, the three psychiatrists were united in the opinion that, no matter what, Archie McCafferty could never again be set free. They all agreed that he was an extreme danger to the community.

The jury chose to believe that Archie was not crazy and returned a verdict of guilty on all counts.

Mick Meredith and Dick Whittington were found guilty of the murders of Ronald Cox and Evangelos Kollias and each sentenced to eighteen years in prison. Julie Todd was found guilty of murdering Cox and Kollias and sent to prison for ten years. Richard Webster was found guilty of manslaughter of Cox and sentenced to four years in prison. Carol Howes was found not guilty on all counts.

Eight months pregnant with McCafferty's

child when the verdict was handed down, Howes made a passionate promise from the dock to McCafferty. 'I'll wait for you Archie,' she sobbed. 'No matter what, I'll always be waiting for you with our child.' She immediately moved into the Blacktown house of Archie McCafferty's parents to have their grandchild.

There was no such lenient sentence for Archibald Beattie McCafferty. He was sentenced to three terms of life imprisonment. Even as he was being led from the courtroom he shouted that he would kill four more to avenge the death of his son.

Archie proved to be a handful for the authorities and he was shuffled around to the toughest gaols in the state. Prison officers and psychiatrists regarded him as extremely dangerous. His one consistent and predominant thought was the killing of four more people. A television crew allowed into the notorious Katingal section at Long Bay interviewed Archie, who told a stunned audience that there was nothing that anyone could do to stop him from murdering another four people should he be let out.

Placed on massive doses of tranquillisers to keep him under control, by 1978 Archie had done time in almost every maximum security prison in the state and was considered to be a gaol 'heavy' and an associate of the hardest criminals in the penal system.

In April 1980 warders foiled an escape attempt by Archie at Grafton gaol. He had loosened bricks in his cell before prison officers were tipped off and his escape route was discovered. At the time prison officers said McCafferty was probably the worst criminal in the state's gaols.

Police believe that Archie McCafferty was a member of the secret 'murder squad' that was judge, jury and executioner behind the walls of Parramatta gaol in 1981. They believe that the group was responsible for four murders within the prison. In September 1981 Archie was charged with the murder of Edward James Lloyd, who was stabbed to death in his cell.

Archie's co-accused, Kevin Michael Gallagher, was eventually found guilty of the murder. It was proved that McCafferty was present while the murder took place and, though he strenuously denied the charges McCafferty was found guilty of manslaughter and given a further fourteen years.

Archie protested vehemently against the sentence, claiming that he had been framed. To prove it, he named those who were responsible to the authorities. Archie McCafferty automatically became an outcast within the system that had been his home for the best part of his life. He was now the biggest headache within the New South Wales penal system. For his own protection he was transferred from one gaol to the next in search of a permanent home.

In November 1981 Archie was caught red-handed in his cell with 110 foil-wrapped packages containing heroin. The judge sentenced him to another three years imprisonment.

During 1983 and 1984 Archie was moved repeatedly between Maitland, Long Bay and Parklea prisons under the unofficial but reprehensible practice called 'Shanghai-ing', whereby senior prison staff were able to pass the responsibility for dealing with difficult prisoners on to others. It was noted in official records that Archie suffered fits of mental disturbance during this period and he was said to be 'off his rocker'.

After giving further information to authorities about serious criminal conduct by various prison officers within the prison system, Archie was eventually moved to the Long Bay Witness Protection Unit in 1987. By now a price had been placed on his head and he was classified as a 'supergrass'.

It was in the Witness Protection Unit that Archie was revisited by delusions concerning his dead son. Prison psychiatrists put it down to the fact that he had been sniffing solvents and petroleum and was extremely depressed by the lack of prospects for his future release. As no parole period had been given, it was clear to Archie that he would spend the rest of his life behind bars. But he kept applying for parole.

In October 1991 Archie McCafferty's application for parole was heard before Mr Justice Wood. The judge granted him a twenty-year parole period dating from 30 August 1973. Archie is eligible for release on parole on 29 August 1993.

It will be interesting to see if the Parole Board recalls that the psychiatrists at Archie's trial might have differed on some points, but agreed that he should never be released.

Archibald Beattie McCafferty is in minimum security at Berrima prison.

4 The Crimes of
Crump and Baker

Allan Baker and Kevin Crump murdered a
complete stranger for $20, a packet of
cigarettes and a couple of gallons of petrol.
They then kidnapped a young mother of three
from a lonely farmhouse, raped and tortured
her as they drove her across the border into
Queensland where they tied her to a tree and
murdered her in cold blood.

When they were finally cornered back in
New South Wales, Crump and Baker had a
running gun battle with police as their cars
raced at breakneck speed along the Pacific
Highway. A police officer was wounded in the
chase.

They could not be charged with the murder
of Mrs Morse in New South Wales as the offence
took place in Queensland. Since they were
arrested in New South Wales, they would have
to be either charged with conspiring to murder
Mrs Morse or be extradited to Queensland

to face murder charges. The New South Wales police wanted to see the case through.

They had already charged Crump and Baker with a number of offences, including car theft, shooting the policeman and murdering Ian Lamb. Conspiracy to murder Mrs Morse was duly added to the long list of charges.

After Crump and Baker's trial, the public was left wondering what would drive men to commit such crimes unless they were insane. But these two men were not mad. Their crimes were premeditated and they merely had to choose their victims. They did this as they went along their path of violence, rape and murder.

By the time they had reached their mid-twenties, Allan Baker and Kevin Gary Crump had extensive criminal records and had spent most of their lives in prison. When they were released within weeks of each other in late 1973 they met up on a property near Boggabilla in western New South Wales, where Baker was working as a farm hand. Crump had stolen a car at Aberdare and collected Baker at the property on 2 November. The property owner last saw them that day and was not surprised at their taking off, as the working conditions were poor due to recent rains.

On Saturday morning, 3 November, forty-three-year-old Ian James Lamb left his home in the central coast township of Gosford to drive to the central west in search of work as a farm hand. His mother helped pack his clothes and toiletries and kissed him goodbye at 6.30. It was the last time she would see her son alive.

On the same morning, Crump and Baker bought a .308 rifle and some ammunition in the farming township of Goondiwindi. Their motive for buying the gun was robbery. All they had to do was find the right victim. It was Crump and Baker's intention that they would no longer work. Instead, they would steal for a living.

Ian Lamb didn't think twice about pulling over to the side of the road and sleeping in his car that Saturday night. The seasonal worker felt secure resting on the front seat of his old car, even though the doors weren't locked and the windows were open to allow in what little breeze there was. He lived hand-to-mouth and carried little, if any, cash. So, he wasn't expecting any trouble.

Unfortunately for Lamb, his car had been seen by Crump and Baker parked on the side of the road near Narrabri and they had decided to steal petrol from it. Allan Baker's chilling statement tells best what happened next:

'We both got out of the car. I got the rifle. I loaded it and I walked over to the car and I pointed the rifle through the window of the driver's side, and I seen a man asleep on the front seat. Kevin looked in the back to see if he was by himself and he was. I knocked on the door with my hands and said "Hey you". The bloke sat up and I pulled the trigger and shot him. It hit him in the voice box.

'Then for about ten minutes nothing happened. It was deathly quiet. I was scared. I then went around to the other side of the car, the passenger's side, opened the door. Kevin opened the driver's-side door and I went through the man's pockets. I got about $20 out of his pockets, it was notes and money. From the glovebox I got some cigarettes, wallet, I don't think there was anything else, but I left it there.

'I noticed that the man had been drinking because there was some bottles of beer on the floor. I didn't touch them because there was blood on them.'

Baker then went on to describe how they had to pull Lamb's body over in the seat and untangle his feet from the brake and clutch pedals before they could drive his car away. Baker, with Crump following closely behind, then drove their victim's car about twenty kilometres from the murder scene and dumped it on lonely Bald Hill Road. Here they loaded Lamb's meagre possessions into their own car and took the petrol from the vehicle by punching a hole in the tank.

In a statement to Detective Sergeant Bradbury, Crump later gave his version of the crime to try to avoid a joint murder charge. He said they drove around and they saw Lamb's car. They then drove back and parked where it was.

'Allan hopped out of the car with that .308,' Crump said. 'He went over and knocked on the door, and the driver's side window was down, when he knocked on the door, and the fellow in the car said "Ahh" and Allan put the gun up through the window and shot him. Just shot him through the neck. Here it was.' Crump pointed to the centre of his throat.

Crump's denial of involvement in the shooting made little difference. Regardless of who pulled the trigger, the jury would hold them both responsible for murder. Ian Lamb had died for $20, his clothes and a few gallons of petrol.

They then planned their next move. They would pay the Morse family a visit at their lonely farmhouse at nearby Collarenebri. Baker had worked for the Morses as a farm hand and had lived in their farmhouse with Brian Morse, his wife Virginia and their three children. He knew that there was a rifle in the house and possibly some money.

On the evening of 6 November, just three days after the murder of Lamb, they camped the night some seven or eight miles away from the Morse farm. At first light they went to the abandoned Mogil Mogil police station, only a few hundred metres from the Morse household. Here they hid their car and observed activity at the Morse farmhouse through binoculars.

Sure that they were unobserved, they walked

down along the river and across a field where they hid behind haystacks. From here they had an uninterrupted view of the morning's routine in the Morse household. They watched as the family had breakfast and Brian Morse worked a short while on his header. When the children were ready for school, Mr Morse drove them down to the school bus before heading off in his truck for a day's work in the fields.

When Crump and Baker were convinced that Mrs Morse was alone, they made their way to the farmhouse. They made no attempt to hide their faces, yet this was the only place in the entire district where Baker was known and bound to be recognised. Was it their intention to murder Mrs Morse? In a later interview Crump said: 'We talked about it on the way down from Goondiwindi and Allan said that if there was anyone on the property they would recognise him and that we might have to kill someone'.

'Was there any further discussion between the two of you along these lines?'

'When we were behind the haystack Allan said that if Virginia Morse was there we would take her with us, and he thought the youngest kid was there, because he didn't know he was going to school. When we got to the shack [the old police station] we put the petrol in my car and Allan said we would have to get rid of her, but we would take her away and rape her first.'

'Was there any discussion as to how she would be killed?'

'Yes. We had the guns so we would shoot her. When we got to the river, Allan said that I would have to prove myself and shoot her.'

In a record of interview with Detective Sergeant McDonald, Baker told what happened at the farmhouse:

'I went to the laundry door and waited near the lounge-room door and not knowing if anyone was home, I asked Kevin to go around the back door and knock and Mrs Morse came to the back door where Kevin was and I was behind Mrs Morse with a rifle. I said "Don't turn around". And she did. I took her in the bedroom and tied her up and she asked me what I wanted and I said I wanted money.'

After they had searched the house, where they found a .222 rifle and a small sum of money, Baker and Crump bundled Mrs Morse into her family sedan and drove it to the old police station where they took petrol from it and transferred everything into their vehicle. The bound and gagged Mrs Morse was dumped on the back seat. Baker told police in a later interview that they had every intention of killing Mrs Morse. And if necessary, they would use her as a human shield to protect them from police bullets.

Crump and Baker decided to head north, over the border and into Queensland. They stopped at hotels and garages along the way and bought beer and petrol with the $30 they had stolen from the Morse homestead. They drove mainly at night to avoid detection. During the 200-kilometre journey Mrs Morse sobbed and pleaded for her life while Crump and Baker took it in turns to rape her.

In a record of interview with Detective McDonald, Baker said: 'We took her gag off and she kept on saying: "What's going to happen to me? My children will be home from school and waiting for me now. I love my children — please let me go home." I just told her to shut up.'

Crump and Baker pulled up at a clearing just short of the Queensland border. Here they 'staked out' Mrs Morse with tow ropes tied to trees and each of the men raped her again. The Crown then alleged that the two men took Mrs Morse on into Queensland, where they stopped by the Weir River. There they raped her again. To a hushed courtroom the prosecutor read of the last minutes of Mrs Virginia Gai Morse's life from Allan Baker's statement:

'She wasn't tied to the tree, her hands were tied in front of her with handkerchiefs, she wasn't crying because I think she was beyond that, she'd been crying most of the time she was gagged and blindfolded. I aimed at her with the .308 and Kevin had the .222 and it was going to be like a firing squad and Kevin pulled the trigger and she fell to the ground before I could pull the trigger of my gun. If he hadn't of shot her, I would because we both decided to kill her because we done those terrible things to her and she would have been able to identify me because I used to work for her husband and I knew if she reported me we would be in a lot of trouble and she just had to be shot.'

Kevin Crump gave a different version of the killing. 'I was forced to kill Mrs Morse by Baker, because he wanted me to be in as deep as him. He said he was going to kill me if I didn't. I admit that I was prepared to kidnap Mrs Morse and even to sleep with her, but once again, as with Mr Lamb I did not want to be a part of her death.

'On the day that Mrs Morse died, she was tied up, blindfolded and gagged by Baker. He told me to go down to the tree and pick up a .222. At this time Baker was pointing his rifle at me. He said to go down to the tree; this was where Mrs Morse was sitting. He said if I did not kill her he would kill me. I was forced to stand in front of Mrs Morse and Baker was saying "Go on, go on", and waving his gun at me. I took aim at her but I just couldn't shoot her. I more or less dropped the gun to the ground and Baker started to wave his gun at me again. He said if I did not kill her he would shoot me. He started to say "Go on, go on" again. I picked up the gun and took aim again. I just stood there for a while and Baker again said if I did not kill Mrs Morse he would kill me, and I believed him. I took aim at her. I fired once. I shot her in the right side of the nose and killed her. I dropped the gun to the ground and I walked to a raised portion of the ground about 100 metres from where I was standing in front of Mrs Morse. I just stood there for a while and I drank a stubbie of beer. I was dazed. When I came back down Baker had her clothes off and he started to drag her towards the river. I said to him "Don't drag her, I will help you carry her".

'It was a choice of either me or Mrs Morse. In fact, a couple of hours before Mrs Morse died she said to me "Are you going to kill me?" and I said "No" because I had no intentions of doing that. The only reason I took Mrs Morse from her property was because if we had left her at her home she would have told police that we had robbed her place, and we needed her as a hostage to get away from the farm.

'I admit that in some way or another I am partly responsible for these two deaths, but I am not guilty of murder or conspiracy to murder.'

Crime reporter Joe Morris recalled the court's reaction to this first-hand account of the last minutes in the life of Virginia Morse:

'There was a stunned silence. Women were sobbing and Mr Brian Morse sat there with his head in his hands. Crump and Baker were smirking at each other. They thought that it was a great joke.

Crump and Baker finally hid Mrs Morse's body in the shallows of the Weir River and covered her with tree branches and leaves. They then headed south to Sydney. On 13 November 1973 their car was recognised in Maitland, near Newcastle, as the one that Crump had stolen from the area on 30 October and the police were notified.

By now Lamb's body had been discovered and police had found the Morse family car at the old Mogil Mogil police station. The stolen car matched the description of a car seen in the vicinity of the Lamb murder and the police were told to approach with extreme caution. It turned out to be good advice.

Constable Millward was the driver of a police car at about 11 a.m. on 13 November. He had with him Senior Constable Jones. They saw Crump and Baker's Holden proceeding towards Maitland, followed by a police Torana driven by Constable Neale. Neale drove alongside the car containing Crump and Baker and they saw him forced off the road.

Millward and Jones then closed up on the fugitives' car, drew alongside it and called upon them to stop. The vehicle accelerated away, with the police in hot pursuit. Baker then opened fire on the police car through the rear window of the Holden with a .308 rifle and struck the police car. Constable Millward closed the distance between the vehicles until Crump and Baker's car was within range of Constable Jones' service pistol. He opened fire on the fleeing vehicle.

As the police car further closed the gap, Baker returned the fire and shot Constable Millward in the forehead. Fortunately the bullet did not penetrate his skull. Kneeling on the front seat of the Holden and using the back of the seat to steady his aim, Baker fired round after round at the police. By now another police car had joined the chase. Constable Snedden and his partner, Constable Hore, picked up the chase just as Crump and Baker's car spun out and wound up in a lucerne patch on the side of the road.

With guns blazing, the fugitives ran towards the Hunter River. The officers left the safety of their car and, firing as they ran, headed the escapees off to prevent them from getting to the river. Crump and Baker dropped to their knees and returned fire, but it was too late. Armed police were converging on them from all sides and, out of ammunition, the two men surrendered to police. The four officers involved in the chase would later receive bravery awards.

In Crump and Baker's stolen car police found Ian Lamb's worldly possessions. A fleecy-lined imitation leather coat, an air-force type kitbag, a pair of tan shorts, some salt tablets, a mosquito coil, a toilet bag, a brown bag, some toilet articles and his shaving gear.

Crump and Baker made statements about their involvement in the Lamb killing but both denied any knowledge of the disappearance of Mrs Morse, whose body had not yet been found.

Ironically, Lamb's body had been discovered on 7 November, the same day that Crump and Baker had kidnapped Mrs Morse.

On 14 November, while being interviewed by Detective Sergeants Doyle and Campbell, it was again put to Kevin Crump: 'I am going to ask you a number of questions in relation to the disappearance of a woman named Virginia Gai Morse from her home in Banarway on the 7th of November. Do you know anything about this woman's disappearance?'

'Yes,' Crump answered. 'We took her away and shot her.'

At their trial, Crump and Baker pleaded not guilty to the four charges of murdering Ian James Lamb, conspiracy to murder Virginia Gai Morse, maliciously wounding Constable Millward with intent to prevent lawful apprehension and shooting at with intent to prevent lawful apprehension.

Both of the accused gave statements from the dock in their own defence.

Baker: 'I am not guilty of the charges of murder or conspiracy to murder. I did not mean to shoot the man in the car. The gun was a scare weapon. All I meant to do was tie the man up and rob him. When I went over to the car and knocked on the door I said, "Hey you", and the guy in the car sat up suddenly and made a noise and I jumped backwards and the gun went off. I didn't know I shot the man until Kevin Crump told me. I didn't know my finger had pulled the trigger. I had no reason to shoot the man; he did not know us. As I told the police, it was dark at the time and we had masks on. I never told them that I intended to shoot or kill the man in the car, and I have never told that to anyone, because it is not true.

'I know we are responsible for the death of Mrs Morse. I cannot forget it, and I know I should be punished for that, but we didn't agree to kill her till the day that we actually did it. When the police were questioning me about Mrs Morse, I felt so bad about it, I just agreed to everything. That's all I can say.'

Kevin Crump also offered little excuse. 'I did not kill Mr Lamb. I agreed to rob him. I knew Baker had a gun, I never thought he would use it. In fact, I never intended to do any harm to Mr Lamb except tie him up and rob him. I never had a gun myself, and I never even touched Mr Lamb before he was shot. I thought the presence of a gun would make Mr Lamb all the more willing to hand over his valuables and not make any trouble. I never intended to do any harm to Mr Lamb, and I repeat that I definitely did not think Baker would kill Mr Lamb. As far as the death of

Mrs Morse is concerned, there was no agreement between me and Baker to do so. I was forced to kill Mrs Morse because he wanted me in it as deep as him. He said he was going to kill me if I didn't.'

It took the jury one hour and forty-five minutes to find Allan Baker and Kevin Garry Crump guilty on all charges. Baker showed no emotion at the verdict, while Crump appeared to stare at the floor and shudder. Mr Justice Taylor then sentenced both men to life imprisonment. He said: 'You have outraged all accepted standards of the behaviour of men. The description of "men" ill becomes you. You would be more aptly described as animals, and obscene animals at that. I believe that you should spend the rest of your lives in gaol and there you should die. If ever there was a case where life imprisonment should mean what it says — imprisonment for the whole of your lives — this is it.'

While Mr Justice Taylor was halfway through passing sentence on Crump and Baker, Mr Morse got up and hurriedly walked from the courtroom.

After the verdicts were given, Detective Sergeant McDonald said Baker had shown no contrition for his crimes.

In the early years of their incarceration, Crump and Baker lived quite happily as man and wife at Long Bay gaol's notorious Katingal section. When a Channel 10 camera crew were allowed through Katingal in the late 1970s, the public got to see how easy they were doing their time and there was an outcry. Crump and Baker were separated.

If at any time the Parole Board should indicate that they may favourably consider an application for parole, then the friends and family of Virginia Gai Morse and Ian James Lamb will remind them of what Justice Taylor said when he sentenced Crump and Baker:

'If in the future some application is made that you be released on the grounds of clemency or of mercy, then I would venture to suggest to those who are entrusted with the task of determining whether you are entitled to it or not, that the measure of your entitlement to either should be the clemency and mercy you extended to this woman when she begged you for her life.

'You are never to be released.'

Kevin Garry Crump is currently in the maximum security section in Maitland prison. Allan Baker is in maximum security in Grafton prison.

5 The Mass Murders of Truro

As recently as mid-1992, James Miller was trying to have his conviction for murdering six young women overturned. He admitted that he helped his lover, Christopher Worrell, dispose of the girls' bodies. He admitted that he drove the car when Worrell went looking for victims. There is no doubt about that. Miller accepted the six life sentences he received, and in the thirteen years he has spent behind bars for the murders he has never asked to be released and has never applied for parole. This automatically excludes him from the possibility of ever being freed.

But he has vehemently denied that he is a murderer.

'I was there at the time and for that I am guilty of an unforgivable felony,' Miller has said from his Adelaide prison cell. 'I fully deserve the life sentences I am currently serving. But I never killed any of those girls. That's the truth.'

Miller has been protesting his innocence of murder for years, on occasion backing up his pleas with rooftop gaol protests and hunger strikes, including one that lasted for forty-three days. But he has been ignored by authorities and his conviction stands. South Australia's Chief Justice, Len King, agreed that Miller should be granted another hearing on the grounds that the judge at his trial, Mr Justice Matheson, had instructed the jury to find Miller guilty of murder even though he had pleaded not guilty. The Attorney-General, Chris Sumner refused to grant a retrial.

Miller maintained: 'They can give me life for knowing about the murders and not reporting them. But they charged me with murder as a payback for not informing on Worrell. It's a load of bullshit. At least one of the jurists at my trials knows the truth. In 1987 he paid a couple of hundred dollars out of his own pocket to help hire a lawyer to petition the Attorney-General for a retrial. If a jurist does this, he must have a fair idea of what really happened.'

The only person who could prove James Miller's innocence is the alleged murderer, Christopher Worrell. But Worrell is dead.

James Miller is a homosexual, who has never had sex with a woman. He is also a convicted thief, but he has no record of violence. At the time of the murders he was thirty-eight years old. Protesting his innocence, Miller said:

'Nobody turns into a cold-blooded murderer overnight or helps commit murder. I'm just an ordinary thief, no killer. I have never been a violent man.'

The Truro murders are among the most infamous of Australian mass murders. Seven young women disappeared in the fifty-one days between 23 December 1976 and 12 February 1977. The skeletal remains of four of the victims were discovered in bush graves over a twelve-month period in 1978–79 in the Truro district, eighty kilometres north-east of Adelaide. What was left of Veronica Knight was found by a mushroomer, William Thomas, on 25 April 1978, in a remote paddock off Swamp Road.

Mr Thomas said he had seen a leg bone with a shoe attached which he had thought to be the leg of a cow. He had thought about the find for five days and had returned on Anzac Day with his wife to check. He had turned over the bone and seen skin in good condition and toenails painted with nail polish. After he had found a skull, other bones, a bloodstain on the ground and items of clothing, he had contacted police.

Swamp Road is so named because it divides a huge flood plain into two tree-dotted flat paddocks. The area's only permanent inhabitants are mosquitos and frogs and the only sign that humans have ever been near the area is the barbed-wire fence running along the

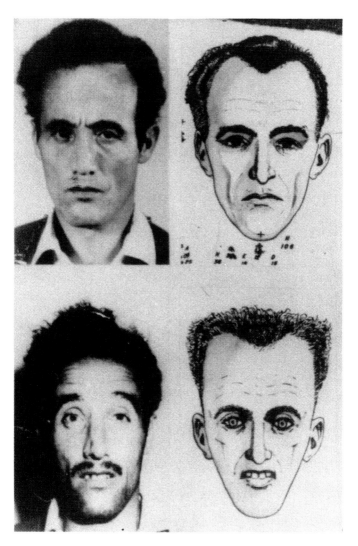

The police Identikit drawings that brought about the capture of William 'The Mutilator' MacDonald. Note the incredible likeness supplied by the eyewitness. This was the first time that the recently introduced Identikit had proved successful.

Detectives bring William 'The Mutilator' MacDonald in for questioning after his arrest in Melbourne. He was later charged with the murders of four derelicts.

TOP LEFT: *The handsome schoolgirl murderer and rapist, Lenny Lawson, after his arrest at Moss Vale in NSW.*

TOP RIGHT: *Lenny Lawson in 1988 at Grafton Prison in NSW.*

BOTTOM: *While in prison Lenny Lawson showed extraordinary talent as an artist and at one stage his paintings were considered for the Archibald Prize for portrait painting.*

Australia's Charles Manson, Archibald Beattie McCafferty, is led into court to face three murder charges. McCafferty had sworn to kill four more innocent people.

*TOP LEFT AND TOP RIGHT: Police mugshots of the rapists
and sex killers, Allan Baker (left) and Kevin Gary Crump.
Both men had extensive criminal records before their
murder convictions.*
*BOTTOM: Baker and Crump are led from Maitland court
after being charged with numerous crimes, including
murder and conspiracy to murder.*

TOP LEFT: *Truro mass murderer, James Miller, leads police to the grave of one of the seven victims.*
TOP RIGHT: *A detective examines one of the shallow Truro graves for clues.*
BOTTOM: *The only known photo of Truro sex murderer, Christopher Worrell, who was killed in a car accident before his victims' bodies were discovered.*

TOP LEFT: *Mass murderer and rapist, David Birnie is led from court after being sentenced 'never to be released'.*

TOP RIGHT: *The grave of Denise Brown who was bashed to death with an axe by the Birnies in Wanneroo pine plantation.*

BOTTOM: *An army of policewomen surround Catherine Birnie as she is led from court after her conviction on four counts of murder.*

Four of the gang who murdered Anita Cobby. Top left: John Raymond Travers. Top right: Michael James Murdoch. Bottom left: Leslie Joseph Murphy. Bottom right: Gary Steven Murphy.

The beautiful young nursing sister, Anita Cobby, having tea with the then Premier of NSW, Mr Neville Wran, after winning a beauty contest in Sydney.

Gary Stephen Murphy was so frightened when police arrested him that he wet his pants.

TOP: *Valmae Faye Beck is surrounded by detectives as she is brought in for questioning about the murder of Sian Kingi.*
BOTTOM: *Child murderer, Barrie John Watts, is led into court to face charges of abduction and murder.*

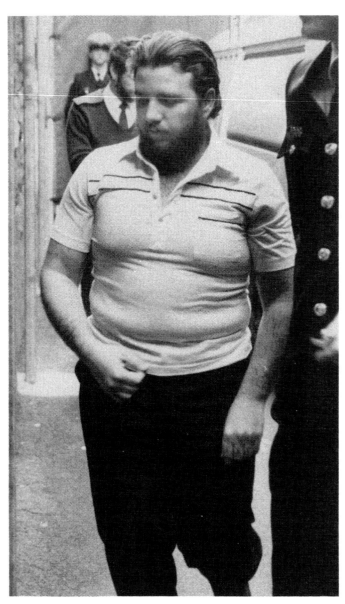

Multiple rapist and sex murderer, Darren Osborne, is led from the court to spend the rest of his life in prison after being convicted of his crimes.

TOP LEFT: Stephen Wayne (Shorty) Jamieson.
TOP RIGHT: Matthew James Elliott.
BOTTOM: The Sutherland railway station carpark where Janine Balding was abducted in broad daylight by the teenage gang of murderers.

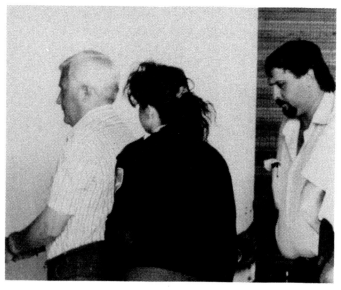

TOP LEFT: The Granny Killer, John Wayne Glover.
TOP RIGHT: Glover's suicide note. 'No more grannies.'
BOTTOM: The Granny Killer is led away to prison to start his six life sentences for murder. John Wayne Glover will never be released to kill old ladies again.

TOP: *Barrie Gordon Hadlow in 1962 after being convicted of the rape and murder of a five-year-old girl. Incredibly, Hadlow would be released to kill again.*

BOTTOM: *Child murderer, Barrie Gordon Hadlow (centre), was a popular member of the local darts club.*

The Carbon Copy Killer, Barrie Gordon
Hadlow, is taken away to prison after his 1991 conviction
of the rape and murder of a nine-year-old girl.

roadside. It is a perfect place to hide a body. You would only come across it by accident. When the mushroomer reported the find, police searched the area thoroughly and found personal effects that would help them identify the victim. There was no reason for them to suspect that there were more bodies in the soggy paddock.

Almost a year later on 15 April 1979, four young bushwalkers discovered a skeleton in the same paddock about a kilometre up Swamp Road from the spot where Veronica Knight was found. From jewellery and clothing found at the scene, police identified the skeleton as that of Sylvia Pittman, who had gone missing around Christmas in 1976. This was the same time that Veronica Knight had vanished.

Police files revealed that five more young women had disappeared from the area during that period. The officer in charge of the enquiry, Detective Superintendent K. Harvey, said that police had always considered the disappearance of each girl as suspicious and their cases had been under constant investigation. He said that about 3000 people were reported missing each year in South Australia and that, usually, all but about fifteen of them were located. When none of the girls who had gone missing in that 1976–77 period turned up, he knew it was more than coincidence.

Now he had good reason to believe that the

girls were the victims of a mass murderer, Harvey was certain that other bodies would turn up and ordered a search of the paddock by seventy police. 'We don't know what we will find,' he said. 'We will be looking for any clues to the killing of the two girls we have found, but we can't overlook the fact that we may find the bodies of some of these other missing girls.'

Eleven days later Superintendent Harvey's suspicions were confirmed when the huge search party discovered two more skeletons in the opposite paddock. They were the remains of Connie Iordanides and Vicki Howell, two of the missing girls.

The police were baffled. The fact that the bodies had been there for so long left them few clues. The trail was stone cold. They appealed to the public for help. In May, a woman known as 'Angela', informed police that she knew of a man who could help them with their investigations. She said that a James Miller had told her about girls being 'done in' in a conversation at a funeral in February 1977. Miller confessed that he and the man whose funeral they were attending, Christopher Worrell, 'had done something terrible'.

Miller had told her the bodies were near Blanchetown and she had not realised that was near where the bodies had been found until she saw a map of the area in a newspaper. 'I only had suspicions, but suspicions are not enough to go to the police. I had no facts. I suspected that it was the truth and I didn't want to go to the police,' she said. Miller had told her: 'They were just rags. They were not worth much. One of them even enjoyed it. I did the driving and went along to make sure that nothing went wrong. They had to be done in so they would not point the finger at us. If you don't believe me, I will take you to where they are. It was getting worse lately. It was happening more often.' Miller went on: 'It was perhaps a good thing that Chris died'. He also told the woman that Worrell had 'done away with two in W.A.'

The informant said that she had not come forward with this vital information because she did not want to 'dob' anyone in. Besides, there wasn't much point in going to the police as the alleged murderer, Christopher Worrell, was dead. She said that Miller would only be used as a 'scapegoat'.

Miller wasn't hard to find. A derelict, living in the streets and parks, he was detained for questioning on 23 May 1979. Police knew that if they didn't get a full confession, or that if Miller didn't reveal the locations of more bodies, then he could walk out of the police station a free man. There was not one shred of evidence to link him to the killings.

In the first few hours of his interview with Detective Sergeant Glen Lawrie at Police Headquarters, Miller denied any knowledge of the girls or the killings. When confronted with the woman's statement accusing him of murder, Miller said, referring to the $30 000 reward, 'Maybe she's short of money'. Lawrie replied: 'Do you really believe that? Is that what you want me to tell the court?' Miller then said: 'No. On second thoughts, maybe she's done what I should do. Can I have a few minutes to think about it?'

When the interview continued, Miller said: 'If I can clear this up will everyone else be left out of it? I suppose I've got nothing else to look forward to whatever way it goes. I guess I'm the one who got mixed up in all this. Where do you want me to start?'

Miller then continued to make the statement: 'I drove around with Chris and we picked up girls around the city. Chris would talk to the girls and get them into the car and we would take them for a drive and take them to Truro and Chris would rape them and kill them. There's three more. I'll show you.'

Lawrie breathed a sigh of relief as he drove Miller under heavy escort to Truro, Port Gawler and the Wingfield dump. Here Miller pointed out the locations of the remains of three more girls. Forensic evidence later showed that the last victim, Deborah Lamb, could have been buried alive.

Although he admitted in his statement that Worrell had raped the girls, Miller would later deny it. Apart from that first admission, in everything else that he said about the murders, he never mentioned any violence. At the time he maintained that none of the girls had been forced into the car or held against her will. It was one of many discrepancies in his testimony. Understandably, the police didn't believe him. It was hard to believe that seven girls would willingly go to their deaths.

Miller then told the police his story from the beginning.

He had met Christopher Worrell in prison and had become infatuated with the handsome young man with long dark hair and slim build who was doing six years for attempted rape and indecent assault. When he was sentenced, the judge described Worrell as a 'depraved and disgusting human being'. He had served all but six months of his sentence when he was released.

Miller was doing a short term for stealing. Friendless and a loner, he was from a family of six kids and had left home at a very early age. With no formal education, he resorted to stealing for a living and sometimes worked as an itinerant labourer. Worrell and Miller lived together when they got out of prison. They had sex a few times but Worrell preferred women. The sexual side of the relationship diminished and they became like brothers. There was nothing that Miller would not do for his friend, Chris Worrell. However, the relationship was difficult because Worrell was a very strange and moody person. The besotted Miller would do whatever Worrell suggested to stop him from flying into a rage.

Chris Worrell was twenty-three and very good looking. His natural gift of the gab saw to it that he had no trouble picking up girls. While Miller drove him around in his old Valiant car, Worrell would solicit girls at bus stops, hotels and railway stations. Miller would drive the couple to remote spots and go for a walk while Worrell had sex with the girl in the back of the car. Often Worrell would tie the girls up. When he thought that they would be finished Miller returned to the car and drove them back to town. According to Miller's unsigned statement, this happened many times and he had no reason to think that Worrell would start killing the girls.

Worrell and Miller worked together as labourers at the Unley Council and were sharing a flat at Ovingham in December 1976. Every night Miller would drive Worrell to look for girls. In fact Miller was so devoted to Worrell that he often slept in the car overnight while his friend was in an apartment with a new girlfriend.

On the night of Thursday, 23 December 1976, the stores of Adelaide were packed with shoppers buying last-minute Christmas gifts. There were lots of young women about that night and Worrell told Miller to drive around the main block of the city shopping centre while he went for a walk. He often went off on his own. He was quite a while and Miller had to drive around the block twice before he picked up Worrell and eighteen-year-old Veronica Knight at the front of the Majestic Hotel. Veronica, who was slightly mentally retarded, had accepted the offer of a lift home. She lived at the nearby Salvation Army Hostel in Angas Street and had become separated from her friend while shopping at the City Cross Arcade. This was when Worrell introduced himself. On the way to her home, the persuasive young man talked her into going for a drive with them into the Adelaide foothills.

Miller pulled the car into a side track and Worrell forced the girl into the back seat. Miller went for a walk to allow his friend some privacy and waited for half an hour before returning to the car. Worrell was sitting in the front seat and the girl was lying motionless on the floor in the back. She was fully dressed. Worrell told Miller that he had just raped and murdered the girl. Miller flew into a rage and grabbed Worrell by the shirt. 'You fool, you fucking fool,' he yelled at Worrell. 'Do you want to ruin everything?' While Miller had him by the shirt, Worrell produced a long wooden-handled knife and held it to Miller's throat. He told Miller to let him go or he would kill him as well. There was no doubt in Miller's mind that Worrell meant it.

Worrell directed Miller to drive out through Gawler and to Truro, a few miles further on. They drove down a dirt track called Swamp Road and pulled over next to a wooded area. When Miller resisted helping Worrell lifted the body from the car, Worrell again threatened him with the knife. Then they disposed of the body. 'He asked me to give him a hand to carry her into the bushes,' Miller said. 'Her hands were tied. He always tied them. We got through the fence and dragged her under.' Together they lay the body on the ground and covered it with branches and leaves. They then drove back to Adelaide.

The following day they reported for work as if nothing had happened. Worrell, who had been in a bad mood ever since the killing, was back to his normal effervescent self by the time they reached work. They never discussed the murder. Miller didn't want to raise the subject as he believed that Worrell would kill him. Never at any time did Miller contemplate telling the police of the murder. Had he done so, six more young lives would have been saved. Miller's only concern was his friendship with Worrell. In the future, a jury would consider this when they determined if Miller was guilty of murder.

At 9 a.m. on 2 January, Miller dropped Worrell off at the Rundle Mall and agreed to pick him up at the other end. Miller waited for a short time and Worrell returned with fifteen-year-old Tania Kenny, who had just hitchhiked up from Victor Harbour. Worrell had chatted her up in the street.

They drove to Miller's sister's home on the pretext of picking up some clothes. After checking that no-one was home, Worrell and Tania went into the house while Miller waited in the car. Eventually Worrell came out to the car and asked Miller to come inside. From the look on Worrell's face, Miller knew that something was drastically wrong. In the children's playroom he found Tania's body bound with rope and gagged with a piece of sticking plaster. She was fully clothed and had been strangled. Miller and Worrell had another violent argument. Again Worrell threatened to kill him if Miller didn't help him hide the body.

Hiding the dead girl in a cupboard, they returned later that night, put the body in the car and drove to Wingfield at the back of the Dean Rifle Range. Here they buried Tania in a shallow grave they had dug earlier in the day. Miller maintained that he helped bury the body because he didn't want to get his sister involved.

On the way back from disposing of the body, Miller suggested to Worrell that he should see a doctor and try to find out what was making him commit the horrible murders. Worrell told him to mind his own business. Again, Miller could have stopped the murders there and then simply by going to the police. But he didn't.

He later claimed that his attachment to Christopher Worrell, who was the only friend he had ever had, was the one thing that mattered in his life. The killings would continue. And rather than be without his friend, the besotted Miller would allow them to go on.

With the second murder behind them, Miller and Worrell continued to pick up girls every night. Their favourite spots were the Adelaide Railway Station, Rundle Mall, hotels in the city and the Mediterranean and Buckingham Arms hotels. Miller never played any part in the soliciting of the girls. He claimed that he was just 'the chauffeur and the mug'.

On 21 January 1977 they met sixteen-year-old Juliet Mykyta at the Ambassador's Hotel in King William Street. She had just rung her parents to tell them that she was going to be a little late getting home and that they were not to worry. Juliet was a student at Marsden High School and had taken a job in the holidays selling jewellery from a kerbside stall in the city. She was sitting on the steps of the hotel waiting for a bus at 9 p.m. when Worrell offered her a lift.

Miller drove to one of their usual spots along the secluded Port Wakefield Road. Worrell forced the girl into the back seat while Miller sat in the front, waiting to be told to leave. While he was sitting there, Worrell started to tie the girl up. She offered resistance but Worrell was too strong. Miller didn't find anything unusual about Worrell tying the girl up. He had done it to lots of them before but usually with willing partners. It turned him on. It was his kink.

Miller got out of the car and walked about fifty metres away. He heard voices and turned to see the girl out of the car and falling forward to the ground as if she had been kicked in the stomach. Worrell rolled her over with his foot, knelt on her stomach and strangled her with a length of rope.

Miller claimed he grabbed Worrell's arm and tried to drag him off the girl, but Worrell pushed him away and threatened to kill him if he interfered. Miller shook his head and walked away. When he came back, the body was already in the back of the car. Worrell was in a black mood and Miller did as he demanded. He drove the car to Truro but avoided going near the other bodies and went to a deserted farmhouse on a completely different track, away from Swamp Road. From there they carried the fully clothed body into the thick trees and covered it with branches and leaves. They then drove back to Adelaide.

On 6 February Miller and Worrell picked up sixteen-year-old Sylvia Pitmann as she waited for a train at Adelaide Station. They drove to the Windang area where Worrell instructed Miller to go for a walk as soon as they arrived. After half an hour Miller returned to find the girl lying face down on the back seat with a rug over her. She had been strangled with her own pantyhose.

Worrell was impossible to talk to. He had lapsed into one of the moods that always occurred after a murder. Miller didn't say a word and they drove in silence to Truro, where they unloaded the body. She was fully clothed and was not tied or gagged. They covered the corpse with leaves and branches and headed back to Adelaide.

The following day, 27 February Worrell told Miller to pick him up at the GPO at 7 p.m. With Worrell was twenty-six-year-old Vicki Howell. She was older than the others and Miller took a liking to her straight away. Vicki seemed to have a few worries and mentioned that she was separated from her husband. He silently hoped that Worrell wouldn't kill her. She seemed completely at ease. Worrell even had Miller stop the car so the girl could use the toilet at Nuriootpa. A little further on Miller stopped the car, and leaving the couple to chat he went to the bushes to relieve himself. He returned a few minutes later on the pretext that he had forgotten his cigarettes. He was really checking to see if the girl was all right. She was nice. He didn't want Worrell to kill her.

Miller assumed that Vicki would not be murdered and walked away into the bush. Worrell didn't appear to be in one of his moods. When he was satisfied that they had had enough time to talk, Miller returned to the car to find Worrell kneeling on the front seat and leaning into the back. He was covering Vicki Howell's body with the blanket. She had been strangled.

Miller could not control his anger. He cursed and abused Worrell for what he had done. It was not necessary to kill the girl. He could have just talked to her and let her go without fear of reprisal.

After Miller had vented his rage, he went quiet, terrified that Worrell would kill him too. He meekly asked Worrell why he had to kill the girl. Worrell gave no excuse. Instead he told Miller to drive to Truro. Miller was terrified of Worrell and did as he bade. At Truro they hid the body under foliage before driving back to Adelaide.

Two days later, on 9 February, Miller and Worrell were cruising in the centre of Adelaide when they spotted sixteen-year-old Connie Iordanides standing on the footpath laughing and giggling to herself. They did a U-turn, pulled up in front of the girl and asked if she wanted a lift. She accepted and sat in the front between the two men. Connie became frightened when the car headed in the opposite direction. Miller stopped at secluded Wingfield and Worrell forced the screaming girl into the back seat. Miller did nothing to help the girl and got out and walked away from the car.

When he returned to the car, Connie Iordanides was dead.

Worrell had strangled and raped her. She was on the back seat covered with a blanket. Again Worrell was in a foul mood and Miller was too terrified to say anything. He did as he was instructed and dumped the fully clothed body under bushes at Truro. That night Miller and Worrell slept in the car at Victoria Park Racecourse.

On 12 February 1977 they committed their fourth murder in a week. In the early hours of Sunday morning Miller and Worrell were cruising in the vicinity of the pinball arcades at the City Bowl and picked up twenty-year-old hitchhiker Deborah Lamb. Worrell suggested that they could take her to Port Gawler and the girl accepted the ride.

Once they reached the beach at Port Gawler, Miller left them alone and went for a walk in the scrub. When he returned to the car, Worrell was standing in front of it, filling in a hole in the sand by pushing sand into it with his feet. The girl was nowhere to be seen. At Miller's trial, Dr C. H. Manock, the director of forensic pathology at the Institute of Medical and Veterinary Science, said it was possible that Deborah Lamb had been alive when placed in the grave. 'The sand and shellgrit would have formed an obstruction to the airway and prevented air from entering the air passages,' he said. He added that it was impossible to say this positively because of the advanced state of decomposition of soft tissue when the body was found. Dr Manock said a pair of pantyhose found wrapped seven times around the mouth and jaw of Deborah Lamb's remains could have caused death by asphyxia.

If he chose to, Miller could have saved all of the victims' lives, but he said that he was terrified that Worrell would kill him if he did. Miller maintained that he did not see Deborah's body in the grave. But later he would lead police to it.

Detective Sergeant Lawrie said that Miller had said towards the end of the interrogation: 'I know it might sound crazy after all this. I don't hold to murder. I really believe in the death penalty. An eye for an eye. Believe me, I wanted no part of this, it was like a nightmare. Each time we picked up one of those girls, I had no idea of his intentions.'

While returning from Mount Gambier on Saturday, 19 February 1977, Christopher Worrell was killed in a car accident. A female passenger in the car, Deborah Skuse, was also killed. The other passenger, James Miller, escaped with a fractured shoulder. At Worrell's funeral, Miller spoke with a woman named Angela who told him that Worrell had had a suspected blood clot on the brain. This prompted Miller to tell Angela that Worrell had been murdering young girls and that maybe the blood clot had caused him to commit these horrendous crimes. Angela had liked Worrell very much and was deeply distressed by his death.

Angela kept her dark secret until the skeletons started turning up almost two years later. Then she told police about what James Miller had told her at the funeral. In her statement to the police, Angela claimed that Miller had said the victims 'were only rags and weren't worth much'. She also claimed that Miller had said: 'they had to be "done in" so that they could not point the finger at us'. Miller strenuously denied ever making either statement.

After Worrell's death, Miller moved from place to place, sometimes sleeping in abandoned cars and at other times staying at the St Vincent de Paul. He was living as a derelict when police finally caught up with him. With Worrell dead and Miller living the life of a transient, it is possible that the Truro murders would have gone unsolved if Angela hadn't come forward.

At his trial in February 1980, Miller pleaded not guilty to seven counts of murder. He sat quietly as the prosecution tore his defence apart. The Crown prosecutor, Mr B. J. Jennings, was merciless in his attack, claiming that Miller and Worrell had 'lived, worked and indeed committed murder together'. He alleged that it was a joint enterprise that they pick up girls and murder them. 'He referred to the girls as "rags". That was the attitude that led him to throw in his lot with Worrell,' he said. 'No rapist and murderer could have had a more faithful or obliging ally.'

Mr Jennings continued: 'You will never know the truth — but have no doubt that it is a horrible truth. These young women were murdered because they were going to point the finger at the young man who tied them up and sexually abused them. They could also point the finger at the older man who ignored their plight and their terror. If a man assists another by driving him to a place where a girl is going to be raped and killed, then he is guilty of murder.'

It was obvious, Mr Jennings said, that no-one could possibly believe the girls had been willing partners in their own murders and that Worrell had never used any force. This was what Miller would have the court believe. Mr Jennings went on to say that the Crown rejected the claims that Miller had played no part in the sexual prelude to the girl's deaths. He said that three of the victims had been dumped partly clothed. They were Tania Kenny, who was found only in a shirt; Vicki Howell, who was found only in shorts; and Deborah Lamb, who was buried only in pantyhose.

Counsel for the defence, Mr K. P. Duggan, QC, said that there was a tendency to use Miller as a scapegoat: 'He was just waiting for Worrell and there was no joint enterprise as far as he was concerned. Miller had found himself in one of the oldest relationship problems in the world — that of the involvement in the wrong-doing of someone else. He was trapped in a web of circumstance. Although Miller admits that he handled the situation incorrectly, he maintains that he is not a murderer.'

The jury did not agree with the defence and on 12 March 1980 Miller was found guilty of six counts of murder. He was found not guilty of the murder of the first victim, Veronica Knight. The jury agreed that he did not know that Worrell intended to murder the girl.

Mr Justice Matheson sentenced Miller to the maximum term of six life sentences. As Miller was led from the court, he snarled at Detective Sergeant Lawrie: 'You filthy liar, Lawrie — you mongrel'.

If anyone in the courtroom had any compassion for Miller it must have been dispelled in July 1984, when Miller was interviewed in prison after his forty-three-day hunger strike. 'Chris Worrell was my best friend in the world,' he said. 'If he had lived, maybe seventy would have been killed. And I wouldn't have ever dobbed him in.'

The maximum sentence for any crime in South Australia is 28 years in prison. But this, or a lesser sentence, is only handed down when a prisoner applies for a non-parole period to be set. Miller has never asked for a minimum term. Until he does he is never to be released. In Miller's case, his 'life' sentence means exactly that.

James William Miller is in top-security Yatala prison in South Australia.

6 The Couple Who Loved to Kill

David and Catherine Birnie weren't particularly fussy about who they murdered. As long as they were female. Their victims' ages ranged from fifteen to thirty-one. Whenever the Birnies felt like killing someone, they would drive along the highways of Perth and pick up hitchhikers. Their victims never suspected the friendly couple until it was too late.

The lucky ones were put to sleep with an overdose of sleeping pills and then strangled. The less fortunate victims were either stabbed or bludgeoned to death with an axe. All were buried in shallow graves in secluded pine forests a short drive out of Perth. The Birnie murders were the most horrific in the State's history.

When twenty-one-year-old Denise Karen Brown went missing on 5 November 1986, Detective Sergeant Paul Ferguson was convinced that she was the victim of foul play.

He hoped he was wrong, but he also feared that there was a serial killer on the loose. Too many women had gone missing over the previous five weeks, and that type of thing just didn't happen in Perth. Maybe in the 'big smoke' — Sydney or Melbourne. But not in Western Australia.

Denise Brown's disappearance was the fourth in twenty-seven days. But no bodies had turned up. There was no solid proof that any of the missing women had come to any harm, but gut instinct told Ferguson that there was something drastically wrong. The disappearances were much more than just coincidence. Ferguson obtained permission to put more time into the case. He consulted former CIB chief, Bill Neilson, for an opinion.

Although there was nothing to link the missing women, Neilson agreed that Ferguson could have a multiple murderer on his hands. And Neilson should have known. He had been the officer in charge of the hunt for Perth multiple murderer, Eric Edgar Cooke, in the early 1960s. Cooke had ruthlessly murdered six people in a four year killing spree to become the most notorious killer in the State's history. Neilson had brought him to justice and saw Cooke swing at the end of a rope in Fremantle Prison in 1964.

Ferguson's enquiries revealed that all of the missing women came from good homes. It was extremely unlikely that any would just disappear, let alone all of them. Painstakingly, Ferguson eliminated all of the possibilities. He could find no secret boyfriends, married lovers or hidden drug problems that might cause them to disappear.

What puzzled Ferguson most was that friends and relatives had received letters and telephone calls from two of the women after they had been reported missing. Fifteen-year-old Susannah Candy had posted two letters to her parents, one from Perth and the other from Fremantle, in the first two weeks after she had disappeared. Both letters said that she was well and that she would return home soon. As far as her loving family knew, she didn't have any problems. And Denise Brown had phoned a girlfriend the day after she had disappeared to tell her that everything was fine. It just didn't add up.

While investigating the disappearance of Denise Brown with Detective Sergeant Vince Katich on 10 November, Ferguson was told on the two-way radio that a half-naked young woman had just staggered into a Fremantle supermarket and been taken to the Palmyra police station, where she had told an amazing story.

She said that she had been abducted by a man and a woman as she walked along the street near her home in fashionable Nedlands. The couple took her to a house where they ripped her clothing off before chaining her to a bed by her hands and feet. The girl said the man repeatedly raped her as the woman watched. The woman also licked around the man's testicles and anus while the rape took place. The couple spoke of injecting cocaine into the head of the man's penis.

Police revealed later that as her attackers made no attempt to disguise themselves or their address, there was no doubt that this girl was also marked for death after her abductors had finished with her. However, in the twenty-four hours she was held in the house, the girl stayed calm and made mental notes. She was also forced to make telephone calls to her family, telling them that she was staying with friends and that she was fine.

While the couple were buying cocaine from a dealer in the lounge room, she managed to escape through the bedroom window and alert police. Thinking that the missing Denise Brown had turned up, Ferguson and Katich sped to the police station. Instead, it was a sixteen-year-old girl who was able to give a full description of her attackers, along with their telephone number and address.

The girl led the team of armed detectives to an old white-brick house at 3 Moorhouse Street in the Housing Commission suburb of Willagee. It was the untidiest house in the street. The garden was overgrown with weeds and the paint was peeling off the fence. Police quietly surrounded the house and went in.

There was no-one at home. Two detectives hid in a panel van parked in the driveway and apprehended a woman when she arrived home. It was Catherine Margaret Birnie. She told them where to look for the man. Minutes later, other detectives picked up David John Birnie where he worked as a labourer in a spare parts car yard.

The Birnies vigorously denied the girl's allegations. Instead, they claimed that she had been a willing party and had gone with them to share a bong of marijuana. Birnie admitted to having sex with the girl but maintained that he had not raped her. A search of the house found the girl's bag and cigarettes, but there was little else to prove the allegation or connect the Birnies with any of the other missing women.

Knowing that they needed a confession to confirm their suspicions, Ferguson and Katich hoped that under intense questioning one of the Birnies would crack and at least admit to the rape of the young girl. It was her word against theirs. Ferguson and Katich grilled the Birnies separately. It was David Birnie who eventually cracked.

Early on the evening of 10 November, Detective Sergeant Katich said to David Birnie, half jokingly: 'It's getting dark. Best we take the shovel and dig them up.'

To his astonishment, Birnie replied: 'Okay. There's four of them.'

When told of her lover's confession, Catherine Birnie also broke. They would take police to the bodies, which were buried not far from the city. It was as though it was a load off David Birnie's mind. He spoke freely with the detectives as he directed the convoy of vehicles out of the metropolitan area and towards the State Forest, north of the city.

The convoy moved along Wanneroo Road and through the pine forests. Birnie was chatting so much that they were almost at Yanchep before he realised that they had gone too far and instructed them to turn around and go back. Squinting into the darkness, David Birnie recognised a track that led off the highway and into the darkness of the Gnangara pine plantation. About 400 metres into the forest, Birnie instructed them to stop. He pointed to a mound of sand. 'Dig there,' he said.

Within minutes, police had uncovered the corpse of Denise Karen Brown who had been reported missing only five days earlier.

With a guard placed around the shallow grave, Birnie directed the convoy south to the Glen Eagle Picnic Area on the Albany Highway near Armadale. After travelling for half an hour, Birnie guided police into the forest and along a narrow track. Up an incline about forty metres from the track, police uncovered the decomposing body of twenty-two-year-old Mary Frances Neilson, who had gone missing on 6 October.

A further kilometre down the track, David Birnie pointed out the burial site of fifteen-year-old Susannah Candy who hadn't been seen since 19 October. Detective Sergeant Katich was amazed that neither of the Birnies showed any emotion or embarrassment while the bodies were being uncovered. If anything, they appeared to enjoy being the centre of attention as they pointed the graves out to police.

Then Catherine Birnie said that it was her turn. She would like to indicate the position of the next grave. She pointed out that it was where they had buried thirty-one-year-old Noelene Patterson who they had kidnapped and murdered on 30 October. Catherine Birnie went to great lengths to explain to police that she disliked Noelene from the moment that she and David had abducted her. She was glad that she was dead. As she pointed out the grave to police, she spat on it. She showed a great deal of pride in being able to find the grave unassisted. It was as if she didn't want David Birnie to get all of the credit.

As they left the burial grounds, David Birnie commented to Katich: 'What a pointless loss of young life.'

There was absolutely no doubt in the big detective's mind that if the young girl hadn't escaped earlier in the day, the killings would have gone on.

Psychiatrists attached to the case agreed that

Catherine Birnie could not have killed on her own. She just wasn't the type. But the quiet mother of six children was totally obsessed with David Birnie and would do anything for him. Including murder. She was even prepared to take her own life for him. When he got too fond of one of their victims, Catherine turned the knife on herself and said that she would rather die by her own hand than see him fall in love with anyone else.

David Birnie was a completely different story. The product of a desperately poor family, he had been in and out of institutions and prison all of his life and was always going to end up in gaol for a long time. But no-one could possibly have forecast the magnitude of his crimes.

David John Birnie was the eldest of six children. Margaret and John Birnie did their best for their kids but times were tough. For all of their young lives, the authorities periodically took the children away from their parents and placed them in government institutions. David Birnie's parents had a long history of chronic alcoholism. At the time of the murders, David Birnie's mother was living in destitute squalor. Her tiny apartment was overflowing with food scraps, dirty dishes, full ashtrays and broken furniture. The place was covered in dust and grime. She had given up hope years ago and could not recall seeing her eldest son in years. David Birnie's father died in 1986 after a long illness.

Catherine and David first met as youngsters when their families lived next door to each other. Catherine's life was also one of doom and despair. Her mother died when Catherine was ten months old and the infant was taken to live in South Africa with her father. She was bundled back to Australia after two years and was fostered by her grandparents. A sad little girl who rarely smiled, she had no friends. Other children weren't allowed to play with her, and even before she reached high school her mind was scarred by loneliness. She desperately wanted to be loved. She would find that love in David Birnie later on in her sad life. But it would drive her to a loneliness and despair that she never knew was possible.

David Birnie was reunited with Catherine when they were both in their late teens. David already had an extensive record for juvenile offences. The only time that he showed that he might make something of himself was in the early 1960s, when he trained as an apprentice jockey. But like most things in David Birnie's life, that didn't last long. Trainer Eric Parnham recalled Birnie as a pale, sickly-looking boy who he took on, just to give him a job. Birnie was recommended as an apprentice prospect and Parnham went to pick the boy up at his home. The house was a derelict slum surrounded by a pack of dogs. Birnie stayed in the stables for almost a year and showed enough ability to become a good jockey.

Parnham eventually sacked him when he was alleged to have bashed and robbed the elderly owner of a boarding house.

Catherine found a friend in Birnie. She would do anything he desired and together they went on a crime rampage that would land them both in gaol.

On 11 June 1969 David and Catherine pleaded guilty in the Perth Police Court to eleven charges of breaking, entering and stealing goods worth nearly $3000. The court was told that Catherine was pregnant to another man. They admitted to stealing oxyacetylene equipment and using it to try to crack a safe at the Waverly drive-in theatre. Catherine was placed on probation and Birnie was sent to gaol for nine months.

On 9 July 1969 they were committed for trial in the Supreme Court on eight further charges of breaking, entering and stealing. They pleaded guilty and Birnie had three years imprisonment added to his sentence. Catherine was put on probation for a further four years.

On 21 June 1970 Birnie broke out of Karnet prison and teamed up with Catherine again. When they were apprehended on 10 July they were charged on fifty-three counts of stealing, receiving, breaking and entering, being unlawfully on premises, unlawfully driving motor vehicles and unlawfully using vehicles. In their possession police found clothing, wigs, bedding, radios, food, books, 100 sticks of gelignite, 120 detonators and three fuses. Catherine admitted that she knew that she had done wrong but said that she loved Birnie so much that there was nothing that she wouldn't do for him. She would get her chance to prove this in the years to come.

Birnie was sentenced to two and a half years in prison and Catherine received six months. Her newborn baby was taken from her by welfare workers and held until her release. Out of prison a few months later and away from the evil influence of David Birnie, Catherine went to work as a live-in domestic for a family in Fremantle. For the first time in her life, the scrawny, flat-chested young woman seemed to have found some happiness. Donald, the son of the family she worked for, fell in love with her and they married on 31 May 1972. It was also Catherine's twenty-first birthday. Shortly after she gave birth to the first of their six children. They named the baby boy 'Little Donny' after his father. Seven months later Donny was killed when he was crushed to death by a car in front of his mother. Psychiatrists would later ponder the significance of this tragedy in the horrors of the future. In the meantime, the marriage was not a happy one. Catherine pined for David Birnie.

No-one was surprised when she bailed out of the marriage. The family had been living in a State Housing Commission home in the working-class suburb of Victoria Park. Catherine had to look after her unemployed husband, their six children and her father and uncle. The place was like a pig sty. She took no pride in the kids or the house. There was never any money for food. One day she rang her husband and said that she wasn't coming back. She had been seeing David Birnie for the previous two years and was going back to him.

After thirteen years apart, she moved back with David Birnie. Although they never married, Catherine changed her name to Birnie by deed poll.

But the Birnie household was far from normal. David Birnie's sexual appetite was seemingly insatiable. James Birnie, David's younger brother, stayed with the couple for a short time when he was released from prison after serving five months for indecently dealing with his six-year-old niece. He told a reporter: 'She [the six-year-old] led me on. You don't know what they can be like... When I left prison, I had nowhere to go. I couldn't go back to my mother's place because I had assaulted her and there was a restraining order out against me. I had a couple of fights with mum and the police chased me off. Mum has alcohol problems. So David and Catherine let me move in. They weren't real happy about it and David kept saying that he was going to kill me to keep me in line.'

James added that David Birnie had few friends, was heavily into kinky sex and had a big pornographic video collection. 'He has to have sex four or five times a day,' James said of his brother. 'I saw him use a hypodermic of that stuff you have when they're going to put stitches in your leg. It makes you numb. He put the needle in his penis. Then he did it [had sex]. David has had many women. He always has someone.'

The killings started in 1986. David and Catherine Birnie had tried everything sexually together and they wanted new kicks. They discussed abduction and rape. Birnie turned his accomplice on by telling her that she would achieve incredible orgasms by watching him penetrate another woman who was bound and gagged. Catherine fantasised about licking Birnie's genitals while his penis went in and out of another woman. She would then pull it out of the woman's vagina and take it in her mouth as he finished.

Their first opportunity came on 6 October 1986 when twenty-two-year-old student, Mary Neilson, turned up at the Birnie house to buy some car tyres. She had approached Birnie at his work at the spare parts yard and he had suggested that she call by his house for a better bargain.

Mary was studying psychology at the University of Western Australia and worked part-time at a suburban delicatessen. She was hoping to take a job as a counsellor with the Community Welfare Department. Her parents

were both TAFE lecturers and were on holiday
in the UK when their daughter disappeared.
Mary was last seen leaving the shop on Monday 6 October to attend a university lecture ...
but she never made it. Her Galant sedan was
found six days later left in a riverside car park
opposite police headquarters. David Birnie
had driven it there. It was as if he was leaving
a clue.

As Mary Neilson entered the Birnie house,
she was seized at knife point, bound and
gagged and chained to the bed. Catherine Birnie watched as her lover repeatedly raped the
girl. She asked him questions about what
turned him on the most. This way she would
know what to do to excite him.

Catherine knew that Mary Neilson would
eventually have to die. But it was something
that she and Birnie hadn't yet discussed. That
night they took the girl to the Gleneagles
National Park, where Birnie raped her again
then wrapped a nylon cord around her neck
and slowly tightened it with a tree branch.
Mary Neilson choked to death at his feet.
Birnie then stabbed her through the body and
buried her in a shallow grave. He told Catherine that the stab wound would allow any
gases to escape as the body decomposed. He
had read it somewhere in a book.

The second killing took place a fortnight
later when they abducted pretty fifteen-year-
old Susannah Candy as she hitchhiked along

the Stirling Highway in Claremont. An outstanding student at the Hollywood High School, Susannah lived at home in Nedlands with her parents, two brothers and a sister. Her father is one of the top ophthalmic surgeons in Western Australia. After she went missing, the Birnies forced her to send letters to her family to assure them that she was all right. But the family feared for her life.

The Birnies had been cruising for hours looking for a victim when they spotted Susannah. Within seconds of being in the car, she had a knife at her throat and her hands were bound. She was taken back to the Willagee house where she was gagged, chained to the bed and raped.

After Birnie had finished raping the girl, Catherine Birnie got into the bed with them. She now knew that this turned her lover on. When they had satiated their lust, Birnie tried to strangle the girl with the nylon cord, but she became hysterical and went berserk. The Birnies forced sleeping pills down her throat to calm her down. Once Susannah was asleep, David put the cord around her neck and told Catherine to prove her undying love for him by murdering the girl.

Catherine obliged willingly. She tightened the cord slowly around the young girl's neck until she stopped breathing. David Birnie stood beside the bed, watching. Asked later why she had done it, Catherine Birnie said:

'Because I wanted to see how strong I was within my inner self. I didn't feel a thing. It was like I expected. I was prepared to follow him to the end of the earth and do anything to see that his desires were satisfied. She was a female. Females hurt and destroy males.' They buried Susannah Candy near the grave of Mary Neilson in the State Forest.

On 1 November they saw thirty-one-year-old Noelene Patterson standing beside her car on the Canning Highway, East Fremantle. She had run out of petrol while on her way home from her job as bar manager at the Nedlands Golf Club. Noelene lived with her mother in the leafy suburb of Bicton on the shores of the Swan River. She was an extremely popular girl and club members described her as 'charming and polite'. She had been an air hostess with Ansett airlines for nine years and had worked for Alan Bond as hostess on his private jet for two years. Noelene had been working at the golf club for about a year when she accepted the Birnies' offer of a lift.

Noelene didn't hesitate to get in the car with the friendly couple. Once inside, she had a knife held to her throat, was tied up and told not to move or she would be stabbed to death. She was taken back to Moorhouse Street where Birnie repeatedly raped her after she was gagged and chained to the bed. Catherine Birnie hated Noelene Patterson from the minute she set eyes on her. A beautiful, elegant lady, Noelene was everything that Catherine wanted to be. What is more, Birnie was entranced by her. They had originally decided to murder Noelene Patterson that same night but when David Birnie kept putting it off, Catherine became infuriated. She could see that she was losing her man. At one stage she held a knife to her own heart and threatened to kill herself unless he chose between them.

Birnie kept Noelene prisoner in the house for three days before Catherine insisted that he kill her. He forced an overdose of sleeping pills down her throat and strangled her, under the watchful eye of Catherine, while she slept. They took her body to the Forest and buried it along with the others. Catherine Birnie got great pleasure in throwing sand in the dead woman's face.

On 5 November they abducted twenty-one-year-old Denise Brown as she was waiting for a bus on Stirling Highway. Denise was a fun-loving girl who worked as a part-time computer operator in Perth and spent a lot of her spare time at dances and nightclubs. She shared a flat in Nedlands with her boyfriend and another couple. Denise spent her last night at the Coolbellup Hotel with a girlfriend. She accepted a lift from the Birnies outside the Stoned Crow Wine House in Fremantle. A close friend said later: 'She was someone who would do anything to help anyone. She trusted too many people. Perhaps that is why she didn't think twice about taking a lift.'

At knife point, Denise was taken to the house in Willagee, chained to the bed and raped. The following afternoon she was taken to the Wanneroo pine plantation. Along the way they nearly picked up another victim. After the Birnies' capture, a nineteen-year-old student told police how she was offered a lift by two people who she later recognised as Catherine and David Birnie from photos in the newspapers. After finishing university for the day, she was walking along Pinjar Road, Wanneroo, when a car pulled up beside her. There were two people in the front and another slumped in the back seat. Later she realised that the person in the back was probably Denise Brown. She went on:

'I felt uneasy. I didn't recognise the car. There was a man driving and a woman in the front seat of the car. The man kept looking down, not looking at me and the woman was drinking a can of UDL rum and coke. I thought the fact that she was drinking at that time of day was strange. He didn't look at me the whole time. It was the woman who did all the talking. She asked me if I wanted a lift anywhere. I said, "No, I only live up the road".

'They continued to sit there, and I looked into the back seat where I saw a small person with short brown hair lying across the seat. I thought it must have been their son or daughter asleep in the back. The person was in a sleeping position and from the haircut, looked

like a boy, but for some reason I got the feeling
it was a girl. I told them again I didn't want
a lift because walking was good exercise. The
man looked up for the first time and gazed
at me before looking away again. By this time
more cars had appeared and I started to walk
away, but they continued to sit in the car.
Finally, the car started and they did another
U-turn and drove up Pinjar Road towards the
pine plantation. It wasn't until I saw a really
good photo of Catherine Birnie that I realised
who they were. Somebody must have been
looking after me that day. I don't know what
would have happened to me if I had got into
that car.'

Safely in the seclusion of the forest, David
Birnie raped Denise Brown in the car while
the couple waited for darkness. They then
dragged the woman from the car and Birnie
assaulted her again. In the light of Catherine's
torch, Birnie plunged a knife into Denise's neck
while he was raping her. Denise didn't die
straight away. Catherine Birnie, still holding
the torch, found a bigger knife and urged her
lover to stab her again. He didn't need much
prompting. He wielded the knife until Denise
lay silent at his feet. Convinced that the girl
was dead, they dug a shallow grave and lay
her body in it. As they were covering Denise
Brown with sand, she sat up in the grave. Birnie
grabbed an axe and struck her full force on
the skull with it. When the girl sat up again,

he turned the axe head around and cracked the girl's skull open. They then finished covering her with sand.

The brutal murder of Denise Brown had a bad effect on Catherine Birnie. She liked the sex they had with their victims. And she didn't mind the women being strangled and stabbed to death. But after the last murder she decided that she couldn't go through it again. That is possibly why she left their next victim untied and alone in the bedroom.

She told police later: 'I think I must have come to a decision that sooner or later there had to be an end to the rampage. I had reached the stage when I didn't know what to do. I suppose I came to a decision that I was prepared to give her a chance.

'I knew that it was a foregone conclusion that David would kill her, and probably do it that night. I was just fed up with the killings. I thought if something did not happen soon it would simply go on and on and never end.

'Deep and dark in the back of my mind was yet another fear. I had great fear that I would have to look at another killing like that of Denise Brown, the girl he murdered with the axe.

'I wanted to avoid that at all costs. In the back of my mind I had come to the position where I really did not care if the girl escaped or not. When I found out that the girl had escaped, I felt a twinge of terror run down my spine. I thought to myself, David will be furious. What shall I tell him?'

On 12 November 1986 David John Birnie and Catherine Margaret Birnie appeared in Fremantle Magistrates' Court charged with four counts of wilful murder. The public were outraged by the allegations against the pair and a crowd had gathered outside the court. Police checked the bags of everyone entering the court. The holding cell leading to the court-room was heavily guarded by police.

David Birnie was led into court handcuffed to a policeman and wearing a faded pair of blue overalls with joggers and socks. The bare-foot Catherine Birnie was handcuffed to a policeman and wore a pair of blue denim jeans with a light brown checked shirt. They stood emotionless as the charges against them were read out. Neither had legal representation. No plea was entered, bail was officially refused and the Birnies were remanded in custody. When asked if she wanted to be remanded for eight or thirty days before her next court appearance, Catherine Birnie looked at her lover and said: 'I'll go when he goes'.

On 10 February 1987 a huge crowd gathered outside the Perth Supreme Court. As the Bir-nies arrived in a prison truck they called for the reintroduction of the death penalty. 'Hang the bastards,' they called. 'String them up.' Under a huge police guard, the couple were led into the holding cells. David Birnie pleaded guilty to four counts of murder and one count of abduction and rape, thereby sparing the families of his victims the agony of a long trial. 'That's the least I could do,' he told a detective. Catherine stood in the dock, holding hands with her co-accused. She had not been required to plead as her barrister was waiting on a psychiatric report to determine her sanity. She was remanded to appear later that month.

Mr Justice Wallace sentenced David Birnie to the maximum sentence of life imprisonment with strict security. He added: 'The law is not strong enough to express the community's horror at this sadistic killer who tortured, raped and murdered four women. In my opinion, David John Birnie is such a danger to society that he should never be released from prison.'

David Birnie stood trembling in the dock as the sentence was passed. His bravado returned as he was led to the prison van under tight security. With the angry mob calling for his blood, David Birnie put his hand to his lips and blew them a kiss. In prison, Birnie had fewer opportunities to indulge in such bravado. Repeatedly beaten up, he attempted suicide later in 1987 and was eventually moved to Fremantle prison's old death cells, for his own protection.

Found sane enough to plead, Catherine Margaret Birnie admitted her part in the murders and was sentenced on 3 March 1987 in the Perth Supreme Court. She stood in the dock, holding hands with David Birnie, the man who had led her down the path of torture, rape and murder. Throughout the day's hearing, they chatted quietly and smiled at each other as the court was told of their thirty-five day reign of horror. On occasions she would stroke and pat his arm.

A psychiatrist told the court that Catherine was totally dependent on Birnie and almost totally vulnerable to his evil influence. He said: 'It is the worst case of personality dependence I have seen in my career'.

Mr Justice Wallace had no hesitation in handing down the same sentence as that imposed on David Birnie. He said: 'In my opinion you should never be released to be with David Birnie. You should never be allowed to see him again.' As she was taken from the court, the scrawny mother of six took one last look at the man who had influenced her life so strongly and so disastrously.

In the years to come, the Birnies would rarely be out of the headlines. In their first four years apart, they exchanged 2600 letters, but they were denied the right to marry, have personal phone calls to each other or have contact visits. In 1990 David Birnie claimed that the denial of these rights imposed a punishment 'over and above that decreed by the law'. He said he and Catherine were suffering physical and mental torture and that denying them contact with each other was an attempt to drive them into mental breakdown and suicide.

David John Birnie is in maximum security in Fremantle prison. His common law wife, Catherine Margaret Birnie, is in maximum security in Bandyup prison.

7 The Slaying of an Angel

On Tuesday, 4 February 1986, farmer John Reen rang police to tell them that he had discovered the naked body of a young lady in the Boiler Paddock on his farm. He said it looked as though she had been murdered. Police rushed to the scene and found the body of nursing sister, Anita Lorraine Cobby, who had been reported missing by her family the day before.

Anita Cobby had been dragged through a barbed-wire fence and punched, beaten and kicked. There was extensive bruising on her head, breasts, face, shoulders, groin, thighs and legs. Her throat had been cut.

Medical officers believe that Anita Cobby was conscious when she had her throat cut. It would have taken two to three minutes for her to bleed to death. Anita Cobby had also been repeatedly raped.

The only thing that police could accurately

assume at the time of the discovery of the body was that the crime had been committed by more than one person, possibly by a gang.

The murder of Anita Cobby united the public in outrage. Petitions with tens of thousands of signatures supporting the return of the death penalty were handed to the premier of New South Wales. A Sydney TV station ran a phone-in poll that registered nearly 16 000 calls, almost 95 per cent of which were in favour of the reintroduction of the death penalty.

To a bewildered general public it was inconceivable that the perpetrators of such a crime could be walking the streets, passing themselves off as normal human beings.

But they were. Five of them. A gang of gutless cowards who preyed on women and other people's property between prison terms. Between them they had over fifty convictions for offences including larceny, illegal drug use, car theft, breaking and entering, armed robbery, escaping lawful custody, receiving stolen goods, assault and rape. Their leader was named John Raymond Travers.

Although only eighteen, police believed that John Travers was responsible for the rape of at least a dozen men and women. He had been in and out of institutions since he was twelve, when he was arrested for using marijuana. He was an alcoholic at fourteen and did as he pleased. His parents had no control over him at all.

The eldest of seven children, John Travers was raised in the Housing Commission suburb of Mount Druitt in Sydney's outer west. There are many hard-working families living at Mt Druitt, but the suburb also has one of the highest rates of unemployment in the State. It is also among the top five suburbs for house break-ins and drug abuse.

When his bus-driver father, Ken, walked out, his mother, Sharon, couldn't cope. She stacked weight onto her once slim figure until she was in excess of 120 kilograms and couldn't even properly perform normal functions such as going to the toilet or taking a shower. As she got older and fatter, Sharon Travers spent more and more time in hospital being treated for a variety of ailments directly related to her eating habits. It was left to John to feed the family, and as he spent his dole cheque on alcohol he did this by stealing. The Travers household was filled with doom and despair.

One thing John Travers liked doing was killing animals. He would butcher the chickens and pigs that he stole and dress them for his family's table. He had learnt how to do this when he worked for a time at the local meat-works. He also liked having sex with them. Many people had been witness to John Travers having intercourse with sheep, pigs, goats, chickens and lambs. They claimed to have witnessed Travers sodomise a sheep, and as he was about to have an orgasm he would pull the unfortunate animal's head back and cut its throat.

John Raymond Travers was covered in tattoos. He even had them on his penis. But the most noticeable tattoo was that of a teardrop under his left eye, which he thought made him look like a tough guy. But he was only tough when he was surrounded by his gang, who would bash and rape women and homosexuals at railway stations and public toilets.

On his own, Travers was a spineless coward. But to his half-witted followers he was a fearless leader who instigated the sexual assaults and beatings. They got away with it time after time because their victims were terrified of the reprisals should they go to police.

But one victim did go to the police. In mid-1985, Travers and his gang bashed and raped a girl at Toongabbie, a few kilometres from Mount Druitt, and the victim gave police a full description of the man with the tattoo of a teardrop beneath his left eye. When Travers heard that the police wanted to have a chat with him, he and three of the gang fled to Western Australia until things cooled down.

They settled in the seaside holiday town of Mandurah, about sixty kilometres south of Perth. It didn't take the police long to notice the dirty looking bunch of scruffs, led by the facially tattooed Travers, as they drove around the town in their car with the New South Wales plates.

Travers started having an affair with a local seventeen-year-old homosexual and got one of his gang to take polaroid photos of them having sex together. One night when he was full of alcohol and drugs, Travers took the gang to his lover's house and raped and bashed the young man at knife point in front of them. Covered in his own blood from knife wounds and almost unable to walk from his injuries, the youth made it to the police station where he reported what had happened. Police rounded up two of the men but Travers and the other gang member had fled.

Back in Sydney, Travers proudly told a close family associate (who became known as Miss X) of the savage rape. He wrongly thought that Miss X admired him. Many times in the past he had confided in her, and she always made out that she was fascinated with his stories. But Miss X had never breathed a word to anyone. She was terrified that John Travers would kill her if he found out.

Travers went into great detail about the rape of the youth and produced the photos that the gang member had taken. He told Miss X that he wanted to slit the young man's throat at the moment of orgasm. Just like he did to the sheep. He told Miss X how he had kicked and beaten the youth after he had raped him.

Miss X was mortified. It was not a story that could be easily forgotten and eight months later, when she heard the stories of how the nurse was murdered, she would remember what John Travers had told her about the rape in Western Australia.

One of Travers' faithful followers was another misfit named Michael (Mick) James Murdoch. Mick worshipped the ground that Travers walked on. His mother, Rose Murdoch, hated the hold that Travers had over her boy and warned Mick repeatedly that Travers would only get him in gaol.

Travers and Mick Murdoch were the same age and had been inseparable since they were kids. They considered themselves to be blood brothers They even looked alike and had the same hairstyles and wore the same clothes. They put tattoos on each other with a battery-operated kit. A standard joke among their friends was that if it was Murdoch who tattooed Travers' penis, then how did he get it stiff to do it? There were inferences that they could have been more than just friends, but they denied it.

Like Travers, Mick Murdoch came from a broken home and had been in trouble with the police since he was twelve. His first conviction had been for smoking marijuana with Travers.

At thirty-three, Michael (Mick) Patrick Murphy was the oldest member of Travers' gang, but he was by no means the smartest. Serving twenty-five years in prison for thirty-three convictions of break, enter and steal, larceny and attempting to escape, his most recent escape attempt had been successful. And he hadn't even planned it. A situation arose where Murphy and another prisoner were put in a position of trust outside the gates of Silverwater prison and they decided to make a run for it. Mick Murphy had been on the run for six weeks at the time of the murder of Anita Cobby.

Mick Murphy had spent about half of his life behind bars. The eldest of nine children, Mick was expected to set an example for his younger brothers and sisters. But he fell foul of the law early in his teens and was rarely out of prison in the years to come.

Heavily tattooed like Travers, Mick Murphy was a thug who had no regard for anyone but himself. He was known throughout the western suburbs as a man to be avoided.

Two of Mick Murphy's younger brothers, Les and Gary Murphy, made up the remainder of Travers' gang. Both were known criminals and, as the locals put it, 'they had more form than Phar Lap'. Four years younger than Mick, Gary Steven Murphy was an habitual criminal with an extensive record dating back to his early teens. His crimes included car theft, receiving stolen goods, breaking and entering, assault and escaping lawful custody.

Gary fancied himself as a fighter, was always brawling and had been barred from most of the clubs and hotels in the district. Once he had had one too many drinks he would look for a fight. Most times he got more than he gave, much to the delight of the onlookers. The neighbourhood was always pleased when the police came to take Gary Murphy away to prison.

The youngest of the Murphy trio, twenty-four-year-old Leslie Joseph, looked as though he couldn't hurt a fly. But like Mick and Gary, he had a fierce temper and couldn't keep his mouth shut, as a result of which someone or other was always giving him a belting. The skinny little criminal's record included many counts of theft, car stealing and sexual intercourse without consent. It was common knowledge that Les didn't have much luck with the girls and the only way he could get sex was to pay for it or get it by force.

Always a tough guy when his burly mates were around, Les Murphy was frightened when he was on his own, and he lived on the reputation of brothers Gary and Mick. Like the rest of the gang, the tiny Les Murphy had spent much of his adult life behind bars. The brothers had seen more of each other behind bars than on the outside.

When they weren't in prison, the Murphy brothers spent their time around the Blacktown and Mount Druitt area in Sydney's west. With Mick on the run and his two brothers recently released from prison, it was a rare occasion for the Murphy boys to be together in freedom, but that fateful night of Sunday, 2 February 1986, the three Murphy brothers ganged up with Murdoch and Travers in a stolen car and went looking for a victim. They found Anita Cobby. As a policeman said later: 'She just happened to be in the wrong place at the wrong time'.

Twenty-six-year-old Anita Lorraine Cobby was a nursing sister at Sydney Hospital. At one stage she had been a beauty pageant winner and was considered beautiful enough to go on and become a professional model. But she chose to do nursing instead.

Anita lived with her parents, Garry and Grace Lynch, in the modest fibro family home at Blacktown, a working-class suburb about forty kilometres west of the heart of Sydney. Garry Lynch had worked as a graphic artist with the navy until his retirement a couple of years earlier. His wife Grace had been a nursing sister and still did the occasional casual shift at the local hospital to help them in their retirement.

As well as Anita, the Lynches had another daughter, Kathryn, aged twenty-one. Both girls were more than any loving parents could wish for. They were good at school, never stayed out late and loved the beach and outdoors. There was never so much as a hint of drug or alcohol problems. The Lynch family would spend most of their spare time together on family outings. They shared their love of music and sports and spent their holidays boating together on the nearby Nepean River.

Anita was a good student and very popular with her classmates at Evans High School at Blacktown. When she was twenty a family friend persuaded her to enter a Miss Australia beauty quest to raise money for the Spastic Centre. The Lynches turned it into a family affair and worked tirelessly selling raffle tickets at local shopping centres. They raised $10,000 and Anita was crowned the Miss Western Suburbs Charity Queen. Photos of the tall beauty with her dark curly hair, infectious smile and wide eyes appeared in all of the newspapers. She became an overnight celebrity.

But Anita Lynch did not want to be in the spotlight. She could have pursued a glamorous life on the catwalk, but to her parents' absolute delight she applied for a position as a trainee nurse at Sydney Hospital. She was accepted and went on to become a sister. Anita was so good at her work that she was accepted as a sister in the highly specialised field of microsurgery.

While at Sydney Hospital, Anita Lynch fell in love with John Cobby, a handsome young nursing student three years her senior. John and Anita were inseparable. They shared the same interests in movies and music and they studied together. Anita's parents liked John and when the couple became engaged, they agreed that their daughter had made a good choice.

Anita and John Cobby were married in a church ceremony in March 1982. Over the next three years they travelled extensively overseas and lived and worked for a time at Coffs Harbour on the New South Wales north coast. They returned to Sydney in 1985 and within a matter of months the marriage was inexplicably over. Anita went home to live with her parents at Blacktown. The young couple kept their marital problem to themselves, but it was obvious that they were both deeply distressed by the break-up. They kept in touch constantly by phone. But they did not get back together.

Anita Cobby had no trouble getting her old job back at Sydney Hospital. She threw herself into her work to forget the heartache of her broken marriage, spending most of her time at the hospital and in the company of her work colleagues. Sister Cobby didn't mind what hours she worked. When she was working late at night, she would ring her father from Blacktown Station and he would come and pick her up. It wouldn't matter if Garry Lynch was in bed asleep, he would still find the time to collect Anita.

Why Anita did not ring for her father to collect her on that fateful Sunday night, but chose to walk home, will remain a mystery that can never be answered.

After work, at 5.30 on the afternoon of Sunday, 2 February 1986, Anita Cobby and two nursing sister friends went to a Lebanese restaurant in Redfern for an early dinner. Lyn Bradshaw and Elaine Bray had done their training with Anita and they had all been friends for years. They shared a couple of bottles of wine and Lyn dropped Anita off at Central Railway Station to catch the train home. Both of her friends offered to put Anita up for the night, but she declined their offers, said goodnight and walked up the ramp to the station. Except for her murderers, that was the last time that anyone could recall seeing Anita Cobby alive.

When his daughter didn't call that night, Garry Lynch wasn't concerned. Anita often got caught late at work and stayed overnight with workmates in the city. She was a sensible, responsible woman and there was no reason in the world for Garry Lynch to be worried. When the duty sister from the Sydney Hospital rang early in the afternoon wondering why Sister Cobby hadn't turned up for work, Mr Lynch suggested that they try her friends' homes. He was told that her friends were already at work and they were concerned as well. Garry Lynch started to worry. He rang his wife at work. No, she had heard nothing.

Mr Lynch rang every place that his daughter was likely to be. By late afternoon he decided to report his daughter missing to Blacktown police, and by the following day the Lynch family were frantic. John Cobby had joined the search and every hospital, friend and working colleague was checked. Nothing. All the family could do now was wait and pray that Anita would walk through the door.

What the tough homicide detectives saw in the Boiler Paddock on John Reen's farm that day will live with them forever. Farmer Reen told them that his cows had been acting suspiciously and were milling around an object on the ground when he left his property in the morning. When he returned they were still in the same circle and he decided to investigate. Loud yelling and screaming from the paddock had woken him on the Sunday night.

The Boiler Paddock, which is a fair distance from the Reen farmhouse, is so named because John Reen kept all his old cows (the boilers) in it. The paddock runs alongside Reen Road, in Prospect, a rural suburb only a few minutes drive from Blacktown Station. Anita Cobby's body was discovered about 100 metres in from the fence. It appeared that her murderers had dragged her through the barbed-wire fence into the paddock. Since Reen Road was a notorious lovers' lane, a car parked alongside the Boiler Paddock on the Sunday night would not have been unusual.

When Detective Sergeant Kennedy and Detective Constable Heskett knocked on the Lynches' door that day, Grace and Garry Lynch instinctively feared the worst. The burly policemen told them that they had found the body of a young lady in a paddock at Prospect. The body answered the description of their missing daughter. Sergeant Kennedy showed Mr and Mrs Lynch a wedding ring which they identified as being similar to the one that their daughter wore.

The detectives asked Garry Lynch to accompany them to the morgue to identify his daughter.

The detectives supported the sobbing Mr Lynch as he said goodbye to his daughter for the last time.

The detectives knew that they would not rest until Anita Cobby's murderers were brought to justice. Two local detectives, Senior Constable Kevin Raue and Detective Sergeant Graham Rosetta, were called in. Both were street-tough cops who knew the area backwards. From that moment on, John Travers and his gang of savages didn't stand a chance. If it took until hell froze over, Detective Kennedy and his team weren't going to let them get away.

A task force was set up at Blacktown Police Station. Journalists reported the extent of the atrocities to their editors, but the full facts of what happened to Anita Cobby were never printed in any newspaper. *Mirror* police roundsman, Joe Morris, recalled the night. 'We sat around all night waiting for a scoop,' he said. 'But they wouldn't let us past the front desk to have a chat with the detectives. As more information about the killing filtered through, we just stood around in disbelief. I have covered a lot of shocking cases over the years and I thought I had seen and heard it all. But the horror of what I heard that night will live with me forever.'

Police had little to go on. A thorough search of the Boiler Paddock revealed nothing. Although her body was naked, none of Anita Cobby's clothes were found. There was no murder weapon, no motive and no reason for Anita Cobby to be in the paddock at the time of her murder. She had no enemies and was not involved with criminals or drug dealers. There was no secret lover or married man in her life. Anita Cobby was the epitome of respectability. Police kept running into brick walls. They investigated the noises that Mr Reen had heard but got nowhere. Reen Road was popular with lovers and with joy-riders. The noises could have come from anyone.

The task force started the long job of checking out the hundreds of local criminals. Sex offenders received special attention, but again the police drew a blank. Detectives interviewed the two friends with whom Anita had spent her last hours. At this stage no-one was even sure that Anita Cobby had caught the train to Blacktown that night.

Then the first lead came in. Residents of Newton Road, a few hundred metres from the Blacktown railway station reported seeing a girl being dragged into a car on Sunday night.

She was screaming. They rang police and gave the description of the car as a grey and white Holden Kingswood. Uniformed police had investigated the call but a search of the area had revealed nothing.

The witnesses to the abduction told detectives that at 9.50 p.m. they heard a loud scream and ran outside. They saw a man with his legs sticking out of the open door of a Holden car. A dark haired woman was struggling violently and screaming as the man dragged her into the car. They could still hear the woman screaming as the car drove away with its lights off.

Two of the witnesses, Linda and John McGaughey, were horrified at what they saw. When their brother Paul and his girlfriend Lorraine Busher arrived home a few minutes later they gave them a description of the car and then Paul and Lorraine went looking for it. One of the places Paul McGaughey checked was the notorious Reen Road, a couple of minutes drive from where the girl was abducted.

About half way down Reen Road they passed an empty grey 1970 HJ Holden. They thought nothing of it as the description of the car they were given was of an HG Holden Kingswood. They searched the area and other likely spots for two hours before returning home.

Although they still hadn't confirmed that Anita Cobby had actually caught the train home to Blacktown, police had to assume that the reported abduction was that of the murdered woman. It fitted into the time that she would have arrived at Blacktown. But why didn't she ring her father to pick her up? Or why didn't she catch a taxi?

Police were working around the clock. They returned to the Boiler Paddock at night to give them a 'feel' of what may have happened. Hundreds of cadet police were called in to search the paddock with a fine-tooth comb. It proved fruitless. The public support was overwhelming. Hundreds of calls flooded into task force headquarters. Every call was treated seriously and followed up.

Two days after the discovery of Anita Cobby's body, the New South Wales government posted a $50 000 reward for information leading to the capture of her killers. The phones ran hot. But all the exhausting follow-up came to nothing. By now police weren't sure that the woman abducted in Newton Road was Anita Cobby. Maybe Anita had caught a taxi and had been murdered by the driver. They checked out every cab driver in the district.

The following Sunday, one week after the murder, a policewoman re-enacted the movements of Anita Cobby on the last night of her life in the hope that it may jog someone's memory. Constable Debbie Wallace wore similar clothes to those worn by Anita on that night and boarded the 9.12 p.m. train to

Blacktown. As she walked the length of the train, detectives interviewed the passengers and showed them photos of the murdered woman.

From Blacktown station, Constable Wallace set out on foot for the half-hour walk to the Lynch family home in Sullivan Street. Police followed in an unmarked car. A couple of cars pulled up and offered the long-legged policewoman a lift. But they weren't the killers of Anita Cobby. Again, the police drew a blank.

On Tuesday, 11 February, police had their first major breakthrough when a member of the public rang to say that he represented four citizens who had information about the murder but were too frightened to come forward. The man met with police and told them that a man named John Travers and two other criminals, Mick Murdoch and Les Murphy, had stolen a car a couple of days before the murder and had resprayed it grey. They had taken the mag wheels from the stolen car and replaced them with normal ones.

The informant told the detectives that Travers had a reputation for extreme violence and carried a knife. The citizens were terrified that if the information amounted to nothing, then Travers and his gang would come after them. As it happened, Travers' name had come up several times already. The police had been told that John Travers was capable of murder but they had been unable to locate him. Local police had been wanting to talk with him about a rape at nearby Toongabbie eight months earlier. The victim of the assault had told police that the leader of the pack had a tattoo of a teardrop beneath his left eye, but Travers and his mates had cleared out to Western Australia.

At last police believed that they were on the right track. Very discreetly, they started checking Travers' known haunts. They told no-one of the lead for fear that Travers and his gang would get wind of it and disappear. But they needed more information. By this time the State Government had doubled the reward to $100 000. With this carrot dangling under his nose, an informant came to light with some addresses where John Travers may be.

In a dawn raid on a house in nearby Wentworthville, police found John Travers and Mick Murdoch in bed together. They admitted that they stole the car but denied any knowledge of the murder of Anita Cobby. Police found a bloodstained sheath knife that belonged to Travers. Asked what the stains were from, Travers said that he had slaughtered a sheep with it.

At the same time as the arrest of Travers and Murdoch, police had picked up Les Murphy in another raid on a house in Doonside, about three kilometres away. On Les Murphy's Holden station wagon were the mag wheels and sheepskin seat covers from the stolen car. Murphy admitted being involved in stealing the car but also denied any involvement in the death of Anita Cobby.

Les Murphy and Mick Murdoch were charged with car theft and released on bail. Police put a tail on both of them, hoping that Murphy and Murdoch would lead them to the stolen car. It was their most vital piece of evidence, as it was likely to provide the fingerprints, blood samples and clothing that police needed to tie the abduction in Newton Road to the murder and to the Travers gang.

John Travers was held on suspicion of having committed numerous sex offences in the area. These included the rape of a young girl at Toongabbie, eight months earlier. Police grilled Travers about the Cobby murder but he admitted nothing. They knew that without the stolen car or a confession, they didn't have a case. Travers asked if he could have a visitor. He gave police the number of Miss X, the woman he had confided in about the rape of the boy in Perth some months earlier.

When Detective Kevin Raue rang Miss X and told her that Travers wanted her to bring him some cigarettes, she told him exactly what he had been wanting to hear. Miss X had a lot to tell the police about John Travers and they arranged to meet in a public place that afternoon.

When they met, Miss X, an ex-heroin addict, explained that she was terrified of being caught talking to the police. Even though Travers was in custody, she still feared for her life. Miss X told of the rape in Western Australia and of another rape that Travers had told her about. She said that in both cases Travers had spoken of using the knife on his victims in a manner similar to that actually used on Anita Cobby. There was no doubt in Miss X's mind that John Travers was their man and she agreed to help police trap Travers. She would ask him if he knew anything about the murder and report back to the police.

The following morning, Miss X arrived with cigarettes for John Travers and was left in private with the prisoner for half an hour. When she returned to the muster room she was pale and distraught and shaking like a leaf. She collapsed in tears and told them that Travers had just told her that he had murdered Anita Cobby. Miss X made a statement about what Travers had just told her and agreed to visit him again the following morning. This time Miss X would be fitted with a tape recorder.

Not aware that he was being recorded, Travers told all. He boasted how they had grabbed Anita Cobby and how they had raped and bashed her until Travers finally cut her throat. Miss X found it difficult to contain her emotion as Travers told of the night of 2 February.

Police had no trouble in rounding up Mick Murdoch and Les Murphy. They had been keeping tabs on them since they were let out on bail. Murdoch was at home. Les Murphy was found hiding between two women under a blanket. One of the women was pregnant. Murdoch and Murphy cried and blamed John Travers as they confessed to police. Travers was dragged out of his cell and, in light of the allegations made against him by Murdoch and Murphy, made a confession in which he named everyone involved. He made no attempt to deny that he was the one who actually killed Anita Cobby. He was proud of it.

Police informed the media that three men had been charged with the abduction and murder of Anita Cobby. Hundreds of people turned up at the Blacktown police station to vent their opinions as to what should be done with them. 'Hang the bastards. Give them to us for a minute,' the angry mob yelled. As they were driven from the police station to be formally charged at the Blacktown Local Court, people spat on the cars and called for the prisoners to show their faces. When the three cars had left for the court there was applause and cheers for the police. It was twenty-two days since Anita Cobby had been murdered.

Now the hunt was on for Gary and Mick Murphy. The newspapers published descriptions and photos of the wanted men and warned the public that they were extremely dangerous and were not to be approached under any circumstances. Police followed every lead and raided houses all over the western suburbs. But the pair eluded them.

Then a man rang to say that two men answering the description of the wanted Murphy brothers were living in the townhouse next to him. Police concentrated their efforts on a block of townhouses in Tari Way in the southern Sydney suburb of Glenfield, about twenty-two kilometres south of Blacktown. They surrounded the block and waited. When a woman came out, police grabbed her when she was out of sight of the building. She told them that the Murphy brothers had been there during the day but had left. The police didn't believe her. They decided to go in.

With Polair, the police helicopter, flooding the area with its searchlights, police smashed the door to the townhouse down and arrested Mick and Gary Murphy. Mick was sitting down watching TV and offered no resistance. Gary Murphy ran into a wall of police as he fled out the back door. One of the pursuing officers crash-tackled him and the pair went sliding into a fence, scratching Gary Murphy's face. He would claim later that police bashed him. They hadn't. Gary Murphy was so frightened that he had wet his pants.

The brothers were taken back to Blacktown police station and charged with the murder of Anita Cobby. Word of the arrests spread like wildfire and an angry crowd gathered outside the police station once more, calling for blood. As many as 1500 people blocked the streets around the station, waiting for a glimpse of the killers. At 9 a.m. the Murphy brothers were formally charged at Blacktown Court. Armed Tactical Response Group police manned all vantage points in case the mob took matters into their own hands.

At their committal hearing in July 1986, it was found that all five accused had a case to answer. In spite of their confessions and the overwhelming evidence, all had elected to plead not guilty. Their trial, held in March 1987, started in sensation. Minutes before the proceedings began, John Travers changed his plea to guilty. He admitted that he was the one who murdered Anita Cobby and would take what was coming to him.

The following morning there was another sensation when the trial was aborted after a leading newspaper published the fact that Mick Murphy was an escapee at the time of the murder. It was decided that the suggestion that he had been in gaol and had a criminal record could prejudice the jury and deny him a fair trial. The jury was dismissed and a new trial date was set down for a week later.

During the fifty-four-day trial, the jury heard evidence from the dozens of witnesses, but it was the words of the accused, their own records of interview, that would be their undoing. Each statement varied from the others but they were unified in three things: that the police had beaten the statements out of them and they were forced to sign them under threat of death; that their individual part in the crime was minimal and it was the others who committed the atrocities; and it was John Travers who cut Anita Cobby's throat.

From the five statements of the accused, the jury heard what really happened on that awful night on Sunday, 2 February 1986.

Travers and his gang had spent most of the Sunday afternoon and evening drinking at the Doonside Hotel and they were all pretty drunk. They decided to go for a drive in a car that Travers had stolen a week earlier and steal a woman's bag for petrol money. The lone woman walking down Newton Road with her bag slung over her shoulder was the perfect target. They stopped the car in front of Anita Cobby and Travers and Mick Murdoch jumped out and dragged her in. They told police later that there was no particular reason for choosing Anita Cobby: 'She just happened to be there at the time and John [Travers] wanted her'.

Within seconds of being in the car, Anita was ordered to take her clothes off, but she refused. She repeatedly told her assailants: 'Leave me alone. I'm married.' Travers and Murdoch started ripping her clothes off and punching her in the face and about the back of the head. Les Murphy leaned over from the front seat and punched Anita in the face while Michael Murphy slapped her. Anita put up a violent struggle but she had no chance against the gang.

They held their nude hostage on the floor of the back of the car while they pulled into a garage to get petrol with money stolen from Anita's purse. On the way from the garage to Reen Road, Travers and Mick Murphy raped Anita at knifepoint in the back seat while the others examined the contents of her bag.

Halfway down Reen Road they stopped the car and threw their naked victim into a ditch where John Travers, Gary Murphy and Les Murphy took it in turns to rape her. Gary Murphy forced Anita to perform oral sex on him.

The five men then picked the semi-conscious Anita up and dragged her through the barbed-wire fence, causing long, deep cuts to her flesh. The sobbing young woman could offer little resistance. She had been so badly battered and kicked that she could hardly walk. The gang carried and dragged her to the middle of the Boiler Paddock and threw her to the ground.

As Anita begged and pleaded to be let go, Mick Murdoch raped her again while Michael Murphy forced her to have oral sex with him. After they had finished, Les Murphy sodomised Anita. While Travers raped her again, Gary Murphy and Mick Murdoch tried to force Anita to have oral sex with them both at the same time. But they couldn't get erections.

Then Michael Murphy went berserk and raped, bashed and kicked Anita until she just lay on the ground, hardly conscious and breathing in gasps. Les Murphy gave Anita one final kick in the head before they decided that they had had enough.

They left their victim in the paddock and headed back to the car. But Travers wasn't happy. He claimed that Anita would be able to recognise all of them and she had heard them call each other by name. She had to die. 'I'm going to go back and kill her,' Travers said. 'She'll never live to give us up. I'll slit her throat.'

Rather than try and stop him, the gang urged Travers on. 'Yeah, she'll see us all in the shit. Go on, go back and do it.' Not needing much encouragement, Travers returned to Anita, sat on her back, lifted her head back by the hair and cut her throat. It was not unlike what he had done to the sheep in his backyard.

In his statement, Travers recalled that he thought he had cut Anita's throat twice. Forensic evidence indicated that he had. Travers left Anita Cobby lying semi-conscious in the paddock, bleeding to death with her head almost severed from her body.

When Travers returned to the car he was covered in Anita Cobby's blood and boasted about what he had done. In his statement, Mick Murdoch said he asked Travers what it was like to kill someone. He replied: 'It didn't feel like nothing. I didn't feel anything at all.' They decided to return to Travers' mother's house and clean up. During the short trip, Travers went into great detail about the killing. They all laughed and told him how clever he was. Not one of the murderers had a twinge of conscience about what they had done. Rather, they joked about the night's events until they reached the house.

Travers explained away the blood on his clothes by telling his mother that they had killed a dog that had barked at them. Mick Murdoch gathered up all of Anita Cobby's belongings from the car and the gang stood around and drank beer as they burned the evidence in the backyard. Five days later they took the stolen car to a deserted clearing in the bush and set fire to it.

In their unsworn statements from the dock, Gary, Les and Mick Murphy and Mick Murdoch all minimised their involvement in the last hour in the life of Anita Cobby. They all blamed each other. They all said that police had bashed them with torches and fists and forced the confessions out of them. Once Travers had admitted his guilt, each of them tried to unload as much of the blame as possible onto him.

Gary Murphy claimed that he was not even there that night. He was drinking with friends, he said, but he couldn't remember exactly where. Les Murphy broke down and cried and asked God to help make the jury believe that he didn't bash and rape Anita Cobby. Michael Murphy claimed that he only went along for the ride and that he was the only one who tried to stop them from dragging Anita Cobby into the car. At one stage he cried out: 'I am innocent. This is giving me the shits.' Mick Murdoch claimed that he was shocked by the whole affair and he sat in the car and played no part.

Joe Morris had seen many killers brought to trial in his long career as a police rounds reporter, but he believed John Travers to be the most despicable murderer in Australian history.

On 10 June 1987 the jury returned a guilty verdict on all four men after a nine-hour deliberation. Mick Murdoch and the three Murphy brothers showed little emotion as they were led from the court.

The week between their conviction and their sentencing was not a good one for the gang. Convicts do not approve of such behaviour. There is a code among men in prisons. Child molesters and packs of men who rape and murder young women are on the top of the hit list. They are referred to as 'rock spiders'. Every one of Travers' gang was attacked and beaten by other prisoners.

On 16 June 1987, John Travers and his gang were sentenced in the Supreme Court. Hundreds of people had queued for hours to hear the sentence. Justice Maxwell did nothing to hide his contempt as he addressed the five murderers standing before him.

'There is no doubt that apart from the humiliation, the degradation and terror inflicted upon this young woman, she was the victim of a prolonged and sadistic physical and sexual assault including repeated sexual assaults anally, orally and vaginally. Wild animals are given to pack assaults and killings.

'This is one, if not the most, horrifying physical and sexual assaults I have encountered in my forty-odd years associated with the law. The crime is exacerbated by the fact that the victim almost certainly was made aware, in the end, of her pending death.

'Throughout the long trial, the prisoners, albeit, to a lesser degree in the case of the prisoner Murdoch, showed no signs of remorse or contrition. Instead, frequently they were observed to be laughing with one another and frequently were seen to be sniggering behind their hands.'

Justice Maxwell then sentenced each man to life imprisonment and added: 'The circumstances of the murder of Mrs Anita Lorraine Cobby prompt me to recommend that the official files of each prisoner should be clearly marked "never to be released".

'If the Executive deems it proper in the future to consider their files, then I would echo the advice proffered, in a case in which the facts were not entirely dissimilar, by a former and distinguished Chief Judge at Common Law, that the Executive should grant to the prisoners the same degree of mercy that they bestowed on Anita Lorraine Cobby in the Boiler Paddock, Prospect, on the night of the 2nd of February 1986.

'I do not think that the community would expect otherwise.'

John Raymond Travers is in maximum security in Goulburn gaol; Michael James Murdoch is in maximum security in Goulburn gaol; Leslie Joseph Murphy is in maximum security in Long Bay gaol; Michael Patrick Murphy is in maximum security in Lithgow gaol; and Gary Steven Murphy is in maximum security in Goulburn gaol.

8   The Murder
of a Virgin

People were sobbing openly in the Brisbane
Supreme Court as Valmae Faye Beck told of
the last minutes of Noosa Heads schoolgirl
Sian Kingi's life. Beck testified that the horror
she witnessed was so ghastly that she took her
poodle to the other side of the car so that
the dog wouldn't have to watch what was
happening.

So sordid were the circumstances surrounding the abduction and slaying of twelve-year-
old Sian Kingi that it was enough to make
murder-hardened detectives break down in
tears. One of the detectives, Matt Heery, may
never recover from the trauma. It was Heery's
job to listen in on the conversations of the
suspects Beck and her husband, Barrie John
Watts, as they discussed their crime in a bugged
cell.

It was Heery's undercover work that helped
bring the married murderers to justice, but the

170

price was high. Having to listen to Watts tell his wife that he would 'love to do it again' was almost too much for the young policeman. He broke down and it is no wonder that he did. The catalogue of injuries inflicted on the beautiful young girl before she was finally strangled was beyond comprehension. Then Heery had to listen to Watts wish out loud that he could have a repeat performance.

Barrie John Watts was so obsessed with schoolgirls that his devoted wife, Valmae, decided that the only way she could save their marriage was to help him kidnap one. So she did.

Valmae Faye Beck was a frumpy, short woman with bleached blonde hair. She fell in love with Barrie John Watts when they were introduced through mutual criminal connections in Perth in 1986. Both were habitual offenders with long criminal records for theft and petty crimes. They were married in December 1986. At forty-four, Beck was ten years older than her lover. A grandmother, she had six children from her two previous marriages. Her second husband was an Italian who returned to his homeland with their two children when the marriage broke down.

Beck was obsessed with the slightly built Watts. There was nothing that she wouldn't do for her man. Valmae Beck came from a tough working-class background and had fallen into bad company at an early age. But she had been out of trouble for a while and for the first time in her life she seemed to be on the straight and narrow until Watts came along and exercised little short of total control over her. At the time of the murder, Valmae Beck was on bail for false pretences. The alleged offences had been committed many months before.

Watts was an orphan from Townsville who had been raised by a parson in Fiji and then Melbourne. His birthname was Beck, which was the name that Valmae took when they married. He left home in his late teens and moved to Perth where he embarked on a career of crime. He was well known to Perth police and was on bail for armed robbery when he was arrested for the Sian Kingi murder.

In 1987 the newlyweds headed for Queensland and stayed with relatives at Lowood in the Brisbane Valley. Already the marriage was starting to show signs of stress. The amorous Watts was constantly on the lookout for young women and Valmae was terrified of losing him. Watts told her that she could save the marriage by helping him carry out his obsession of having intercourse with a virgin. She gladly obliged.

'He always said that he'd just once like to rape somebody, especially a virgin, to feel what it was like,' Beck said at her trial. 'I didn't feel I had the qualities to hold a man and I was terrified that Barrie was going to leave me for a younger woman.'

In mid-November 1987, Watts and Beck started cruising along the parks and beaches of the holiday resorts north of Brisbane in search of a victim.

Sian Kingi was one of the prettiest girls at the Sunshine Beach State School at Noosa. She was a shy, slender, blonde young lady who loved jazz ballet and sports. Sian was extremely popular with her classmates and had lots of friends in the district. She moved to Noosa from New Zealand with her mother Lynda, father Barry and her younger brother Joss, aged eight, in 1982. She would have turned thirteen on 16 December 1987. Her dad worked as a contract linesman and the young family found the idyllic lifestyle of sunny Noosa to be the perfect environment to enjoy a happy and loving family life.

The tourists flocked to Noosa to take advantage of the beautiful beaches, superb fishing and the laid-back lifestyle that has made the Sunshine Coast one of the most famous holiday resorts in the country. Although only a ninety-minute drive north of Brisbane, Noosa could well be a million miles from the hustle and bustle of a big city. The Kingi family felt lucky to be able to live in Noosa all year round.

On the afternoon of Friday, 27 November 1987, Sian met her mother after school. They had a facial and went shopping together at the Noosa Fair. Sian was wearing her school uniform — sky blue and white striped tunic

— white joggers and white socks and was carrying an olive-green nylon school backpack. Mrs Kingi recalled that her daughter had been a little upset that afternoon. 'Sian seemed a bit worried about something,' she recalled. 'I think it was because she had broken a special vase at home. The vase belonged to a close friend and I told Sian she would have to apologise to her. I had told her a thousand times about the dangers of talking to strangers or accepting lifts. Maybe she was thinking about the vase when the stranger tricked her into getting into his car.'

Sian had her bike with her and decided to ride home while her mother walked. Some of Sian's school friends playing at a nearby tennis court saw Sian riding her bike past at 5.30 p.m. They were the last people to see her alive.

When Sian hadn't turned up for dinner, Mrs Kingi went looking for her. Her bike was found in the Pinnaroo Park, just a couple of minutes away from where she left her mother. A group of people who arrived at 5.40 to have a picnic nearby remembered seeing the bike lying on the ground but did not recall seeing the thin, blonde schoolgirl. But they did see a white Holden station wagon in the area about the same time that Sian went missing. A blond man aged about thirty was also seen in the vicinity. A man of similar description had tried to abduct a nine-year-old girl in the same area two weeks earlier.

Three more people came forward and reported seeing the white station wagon. A distraught Mrs Lynda Kingi told police: 'I can't understand all this. It's completely out of character for her to go missing like this. I'm afraid that something terrible has happened, although I must try to think positively while there is still hope. Sian was very fit. She had no reason to put her bike down in the park.'

Sian Kingi would never have dreamed of talking to a strange man, let alone get into a car with him, but it was not a man who approached her that day in the park. It was a short, friendly woman with blonde hair.

When Sian hadn't turned up by the Monday, six homicide detectives from Brisbane joined the search. This boosted the police team to sixteen officers. Hundreds of local residents joined in helping to scour the area in the vain hope that the young girl was still alive. Police throughout Australia were alerted to keep a lookout for a white or cream 1973–74 Holden Kingswood station sedan. The search for the thirty-year-old man with the bleached blond hair continued.

A mannequin dressed as Sian Kingi was put on display outside the Noosa police station and at the Sunshine Coast Shopping Centre. As the days passed and the search intensified, police gave little hope of finding the girl alive.

At 9 a.m. on 3 December a local resident on his way to work in an orchard found the body of Sian Kingi. He had become suspicious of a lingering smell in the forest and had decided to investigate. Sian's body had been dumped in a shallow creek a few metres from a dirt track in the Tinbeerwah Forest near Tewantin, just twenty kilometres from where she was last seen. It is a popular place with bushwalkers and is a recommended scenic drive for tourists. No attempt had been made to hide the body.

What the police discovered sickened them. Sian Kingi had been sexually assaulted, stabbed more than twelve times and strangled. The head of the investigation, Detective Senior Sergeant Neil Magnussen of the Sunshine Coast CIB said: 'She was lying face up under a tree next to a rainforest stream. She had multiple stab wounds to the chest and had possibly been raped. We found her schoolbag and books nearby. Sian was still dressed in her school tunic but her underwear was found in the creek. It is an extremely vicious murder.'

Detective Magnussen made a statement to the press in which he urged parents on the Sunshine Coast to watch their daughters closely. 'We have a maniac on the loose in the Noosa area,' he warned. 'It is highly likely that he will kill again. No young woman should be allowed out of sight until this matter is cleared up.'

Police intensified their search for an old white station wagon with curtains, a sun visor and mag wheels and the mysterious blond man. These were their only clues. When garage proprietor Darryl Tracey of the nearby Coolum Beach service station reported to police that a bond man in a white Holden station wagon had left a tyre at his garage for repair, they thought they had their first breakthrough. The tyre, with a badly damaged inside rim, could have been damaged as it was driven up the narrow stony track that leads to where Sian's body was found. Police kept a close eye on the garage for the blond man to turn up. He never came back.

On 11 December police at Ipswich, about twenty kilometres out of Brisbane, reported that a man and a woman in an off-white Holden station wagon had tried to abduct a twenty-four-year-old woman at knifepoint at the Ipswich Shopping Centre car park at 5.30 p.m. She had given a good description of the vehicle to the police, including the fact that it had black-and-white registration plates. This narrowed the field enormously and police immediately started investigating the 6000 Queensland-registered Holden station wagons to find the ones with black and white plates that could have been in the area at the time.

The task force combined this information with what they already knew from the murder of Sian Kingi. Maybe they weren't looking for a young blond man at all. The description of the would-be abductors matched that of a couple who had been seen acting suspiciously at the Pinnaroo Park the afternoon that Sian disappeared. But police hadn't been looking for a couple. Not in their wildest dreams did they imagine that any female could be a part of such a crime.

The man who reported the incident remembered the car well. While he didn't get the registration number, he did remember that it wasn't a local car. It was an early model white Holden wagon with black-and-white plates, but they were Western Australian plates. The police couldn't believe their luck. This looked like the breakthrough they had been praying for.

Police abandoned their search for the elusive blond man and concentrated their efforts on the couple in the car with the Western Australian plates. The registration and description were circulated nationally and a policeman remembered seeing the car in Lowood.

Their enquiries led police to the house in Lowood where a couple with a white car had been staying. They had gone on holidays only days earlier, but the police walked away with the names of Barrie John Watts and Valmae Faye Beck, a married couple from Perth who were habitual criminals and were both on bail. Police knew they were on the right track but they still had trouble convincing themselves that a woman — and a mother and grandmother at that — could be party to such an atrocity.

A postcard sent to a relative in Lowood was handed in to the police. It was postmarked at The Entrance, a holiday resort on the New South Wales central coast about a hundred kilometres north of Sydney. On 12 December police raided a motel at The Entrance and arrested Barrie Watts and Valmae Beck, who were extradited to Queensland two days later and charged with the murder of Sian Kingi within hours of being questioned.

The following day a crowd of 150 angry people had gathered outside the Noosa Heads Courthouse. A hangman's noose was dangling from the old building's flagpole and bricks were thrown at the couple as they were led handcuffed across the twenty-five-metre court-yard that separates the police station from the courthouse. Citizens in the street were signing a petition to bring back the death penalty for sex offenders.

People waved placards saying 'If they're guilty, I'd hang them' and 'No air for this pair — hang 'em'. They yelled 'Hang the bastards'. Watts and Beck were formally charged with murder, rape, sodomy and deprivation of liberty.

They stood emotionless in the dock as the charges were read. Beck was dressed in a track-suit and Watts in a blue shirt and jeans. They didn't enter a plea. The prosecutor, Constable Tony Hurley, told the court that Beck had allegedly signed full confessions regarding Sian's murder and the attack in Ipswich.

Watts and Beck were also charged with unlawfully assaulting the Ipswich woman, causing her bodily harm, attempted rape and attempted unlawful killing. This second attack had confirmed police fears that the killers of Sian Kingi would strike again. Beck and Watts were remanded in custody to appear again at the Noosa Magistrates' Court on 5 April 1988.

As the van containing Watts and Beck drove away from the courthouse, people punched at it and yelled abuse. When it had gone they clapped and cheered the police as they walked from the court.

At their committal hearing in April 1988, the court listened in horror as Constable Matthew Heery told of secretly recorded conversations between Watts and Beck as they awaited their trial in bugged adjoining cells. Heery recalled one conversation where Beck said to Watts: 'To commit rape is one thing, but to kill someone in cold blood with no compassion is something else.' Watts replied: 'I wanted to do it again. Remember, you wanted to do it again as well.'

In a statement, pathologist Dr Anthony Ansford told the court that Sian Kingi's throat was cut through to the spinal cord and it was possible she had also been strangled with a rope or cord. He said many of Sian Kingi's wounds punctured her heart and lungs.

Beck did not enter a plea. Watts pleaded not guilty. Both were committed for trial and remanded to the Supreme Court in Brisbane on 3 May.

At her trial on 13 October 1988, Valmae Faye Beck pleaded guilty to all of the charges except murder. Watts had pleaded not guilty on all charges and would be tried separately at a later date. For the first time the jury was played the tapes of the bugged conversation as Watts and Beck chatted and abused each other prior to being charged. The tapes began when Beck arrived back from spending all night with police. She avoided Watts' questions about whether she had confessed.

Beck: 'We're going to gaol for life, Barrie'.

Watts: 'You've turned into a really, really staunch wife. A real good wife, good loving wife... putting your husband straight into a murder rap. That's what you've done.'

Beck then begged him to plead insanity: 'If you listen to me you will get out of it. I won't, but you will. I can't plead insanity but you can.'

After he had seen Beck's record of interview, Watts was not impressed: 'You hung me. Good on you. Top wife. If you hadn't betrayed me we could have got away with it.'

Beck: 'No jury in the land would have found us innocent. You know it and I know it.'

Watts: 'No one seen us pick her up and throw her in the car, no one seen her in the car and no one seen us kill her. I wish I was dead.'

Beck: 'So do I. Have you got any ideas?'

Valmae Faye Beck's statement was then read to the court. She said that on Watts' instructions she spoke to Sian Kingi as she rode her bicycle through the park, asking her if she had seen a small French poodle. As they talked, Watts grabbed the unsuspecting Sian from behind and bundled her into the back of the station wagon. Sian's mouth and hands were taped as Beck drove them to the secluded forest area.

Beck said: 'She was very, very frightened. She was petrified but she didn't cry. I wouldn't have liked to have been in her shoes if I was her age or any age, I suppose.' When they arrived at the creek, Beck watched as Watts raped the girl for half an hour. Watts then forced her to put her school uniform back on.

Then Watts put his knee in the middle of her back and started strangling her with the belt off Beck's dress. 'She was making horrible gurgling noises,' Beck stated. 'I know how the noises sound in my mind but I couldn't describe them to anyone else. Barrie called out for me to help him. I just heard the noises the girl was making and seen her legs moving. I turned away and the next time I looked out of the corner of my eye I seen Barrie stabbing her somewhere in the chest. I took our dog to the other side of the car so it couldn't see what was happening.

'I turned around again and Barrie had his foot in the middle of her back as she was kneeling on all fours. He was strangling her with the belt with one hand and stabbing her in the

neck and chest with the other hand. The next
thing I knew was, he had her face down in the
creek and he was cutting her throat.'

Beck and Watts then drove home to
Lowood, had a bath and watched TV.

Apart from the audible sobbing, the court
was in stunned silence. How a mother of six
could sit by and let that happen to a child
was unthinkable. Valmae Faye Beck sat emotionless as every eye in the court fixed upon
her in disbelief.

The Crown prosecutor, Mr Adrian Gundelach,
told the jury in his final address: 'Now is not
the time for tears for Sian Kingi, now is the time
for justice for Sian and the accused Valmae Faye
Beck. The woman before you is a very accomp-
lished liar who is trying to save herself, but certainly not trying to save her husband.

'Murder was obviously contemplated that
day. Beck and Watts had made no attempt
to disguise themselves or their car. No tape
was put around Sian's eyes, but around her
mouth to stop her calling out. Watts knew
whatever Sian saw it didn't matter because she
wasn't going to live to tell anyone. She was
meant to die and die quietly.'

The jury took four hours to find Valmae
Faye Beck guilty of all charges, including that
of murder. When he sentenced her to the maximum sentence of life imprisonment with hard
labour, Mr Justice Kelly referred to the prisoner as a 'callous and depraved woman'. 'No

decent person could not feel revulsion at what you did — and you, a mother with children of your own,' he told Beck as she sat apparently unaffected by the verdict.

After a long series of delays, Barrie John Watts was finally tried in the Brisbane Supreme Court in February 1990. Although the evidence was damning and his wife's testimony would send him to prison forever, he pleaded not guilty. In his defence Watts claimed that Beck did the murder on her own.

Crown prosecutor, Mr Vishal Lakshman, told the court that it was stretching the imagination to believe that Valmae Beck was there alone. He asked the jury to wonder how Beck — 'no matter what her perversion, no matter how depraved' — could have abducted, brutally raped and murdered the girl on her own. The jury returned with the guilty of murder verdict after an overnight deliberation.

In sentencing Barrie John Watts to imprisonment for life, Mr Justice Jelly said: 'The murder and rape was a particularly shocking and revolting crime which shows you up as a thoroughly evil man devoid of any sense of morality. Life sentence is the only sentence for murder and in your case the sentence should mean just that. In my opinion you should never be released.'

Barrie John Watts is in maximum security in Brisbane gaol; Valmae Faye Beck is in maximum security in Brisbane Women's prison.

9 The Devil Made Me Do It

The coach captain checked the speedo on his eighteen-wheel road liner. No, he wasn't speeding. And he was certain that he hadn't gone over the limit at any time since he had left Perth. Then why would the police want to have a chat with him? He was puzzled why they would radio ahead on the two-way and tell him to call into Eucla for an unscheduled stop. And it was annoying. He was fifteen hours into his journey to Adelaide and was dead on schedule. Still, it would give his passengers a chance to see how remarkable the tiny township is.

Eucla is in the middle of the desert and sits on the top of the huge white cliffs that look across the Great Australian Bight. It is like a strange oasis. As the coach captain pulled into the roadhouse parking area he was met by two plain-clothed policemen who quietly boarded his bus.

'Morning Captain,' said Sergeant George Johansen. 'Sorry to interrupt your trip. Do you mind if we take a look around?'

'Not at all,' he replied, relieved that they appeared to be looking for someone. This was no traffic pinch.

The passengers looked up at Johansen as he moved slowly down the aisle. He hardly spared a glance at the young honeymooners cuddled up at the front, but he threw a quick smile at the two pretty American tourists. They smiled back at the man who looked so out of place in a suit in the middle of the Nullarbor Plain. Then Sergeant Johansen had a close look at the hands of the clean-shaven young man who was asleep with his head resting against the window. No. That wasn't him.

Finally his eyes rested on a young man. Short, bearded and pudgy, he was sitting at the back of the coach. The man was stooped over with his head in his lap, as if to hide his face. Johansen stood over the man for a few seconds, but did not speak. Although they had never met, Sergeant Johansen knew the man.

'Show me your hands,' Johansen demanded. The man complied. On the back of his hands were tattooed crosses. And on his forearm was a tattoo of a stickman.

'Are you Darren Osborne?'

'Yes.'

'Grab your gear and come with me.'

Osborne offered no resistance but fearing otherwise, Johansen had his hand inside his jacket and around the butt of his police-issue .38 Smith and Wesson. The madman could come at him with his knife. If he did, then he was ready. And other armed detectives surrounded the bus. Chances are that the other passengers on the bus that day in May 1987 never found out that they were sharing the trip with one of Australia's most wanted criminals.

Such was the ferocity of the rape and murder of Susan Frost at Albany in southern Western Australia three days earlier that police had prepared themselves for the worst. This was an extremely dangerous homicidal maniac and their instructions were to approach with extreme caution. As it happened, their suspect broke down in tears and confessed his crimes to police on the long trip back to Perth. He begged forgiveness because 'the Devil drove me to kill'.

Police also believed that Osborne could help interstate detectives with their enquiries into a series of extremely violent rapes in Queensland and Victoria. There was also the recent rape of a sixteen-year-old girl at East Perth in which the suspect answered to Osborne's description. In one of the attacks in Queensland, the victim had been left for dead with her throat cut from ear to ear.

When apprehended, Osborne confessed to all of the crimes.

Darren Osborne's career as a violent rapist

began in Queensland in 1982 when he was just eighteen years old. He raped three girls at knife point and was sentenced to nine years gaol. Placed on parole in October 1986, after serving just four-and-a-half years of his sentence, he is alleged to have launched one of the most savage knife attacks in Queensland's criminal history within a week of his release.

Brisbane beautician, Shari Davies, was kidnapped at knife point from a Brisbane car park on 5 November 1986. Her attacker told her to drive her car into remote bushland behind Goodna cemetery on the city's outskirts. There she was viciously bashed and then stabbed twelve times in the neck and body before her throat was slit and she was left for dead. But, semiconscious, she managed to crawl fifty metres to the side of the road where she lay for ten hours before she was found the next morning. Shari Davies hovered between life and death for a week, but she eventually recovered and was able to describe her attacker to police. From the description of the tattoos on the back of the rapist's hands, police had a lot to go on. A massive manhunt was launched, but Osborne had fled.

From her hospital bed, Shari Davies made a prophetic plea to police all around Australia. 'Please, please find my evil attacker before an innocent girl is murdered,' she begged. 'He'll kill next time. He's got nothing to lose.'

When Osborne did eventually murder Susan Frost in Albany, Shari's father, Ian Davies, was extremely critical of the decision to release Osborne from prison after he had served only half of his sentence. He said the Queensland Parole Board had made an error of judgment and should pay. 'I want to make these bastards take more care,' he said. 'There are probably people who have never seen the rough and tough of life and a prisoner who puts a story over to them is let off.' In 1988 Shari Davies was awarded a record $40 000 compensation from the Queensland government.

Osborne next struck on 27 November 1986, when he allegedly raped a thirty-three-year-old mother of two at knife point in the toilets of McDonald's in Swanston Street in the heart of Melbourne. She described her attacker as having tattoos of crosses on the back of his hands. Police knew that Osborne was on the move, but where would be turn up next?

When a man with the familiar tattoos violently raped a sixteen-year-old girl at knife point in Perth on 24 April 1987 police decided to circulate a description of the man and his tattoos to the press.

On 5 May in Albany, Osborne stole a knife, abducted a woman and forced her to drive him to Mount Clarence, a local tourist spot. There he twice ordered the woman to perform oral sex before raping her at knife point. Again the victim described the man with the tattoos.

CIB inquiries led the police to a Perth dropout centre where Osborne had been staying with

a male friend. Here they were told that the two
men had travelled to Western Australia together
from the eastern states. Osborne was travelling
under an assumed name. Eventually the two
men had split up and Osborne had headed south.
Police stepped up their hunt in the Albany area
but Osborne had gone to ground.

Osborne was living in an abandoned, derelict
tavern near the centre of Albany when on
Mother's Day, 10 May, he saw twenty-three-
year-old Susan Frost on her way to the nearby
New World Tavern where she worked as a
barmaid. As she entered the staff entrance at
the back of the hotel, Osborne seized her at
knife point and dragged her back to his car
which was parked a short distance away. As
with his other victims, he forced Miss Frost
to perform oral sex and then raped her. He
then marched the young woman at knife point
to a nearby car park where he raped her again
and then stabbed her to death with a butcher's
knife. Her body was found by a passing
shopper the following morning.

Police were staggered by the ferocity of this
attack. The young woman had been stabbed
twenty-two times in the neck, body, arms and
legs. In his frenzy, the killer had missed her
body many times and there were stab marks
in the ground all around the victim.

Within an hour of killing Susan Frost,
Osborne had buried the knife, washed the
blood off his hands and arrived at the home

of Mrs Dorothy Wray, a woman he had befriended. The deeply religious Mrs Wray had given Osborne a lift in her car several weeks earlier and felt sorry for him. She said later that he appeared agitated when he arrived at her door and after they held long prayer sessions over the next three days he told her of the rape in Queensland and how he wanted to go back and surrender to police. Mrs Wray said she bought him a bus ticket to Brisbane on the understanding that he would surrender himself to police the minute he arrived home.

Meanwhile, the police had thrown everything into the hunt for Osborne. Police officers called at every motel, hotel and caravan park, leaving photos of the wanted man. Detectives were told that he had been a regular at the White Star Hotel and it was there that they were given Mrs Wray's address.

The poor woman was in deep shock when she learned that the man she had been mothering for three days was Australia's most wanted rapist and murderer. She gladly supplied police with details of Osborne's bus trip.

At his trial Osborne pleaded guilty to murder and abduction. He showed no emotion as Mr Justice Smith told him: 'You are sentenced to prison with strict security for the rest of your life. You should never be released until senility overtakes you.'

Darren Osborne is in maximum security in Fremantle prison.

10 The Most Dangerous Man in Australia

In August 1989 Francis James Carter was sentenced to life imprisonment for bashing a man to death with a baseball bat. The victim's 'crime' was that he spoke to Carter's girlfriend at a barbecue. Carter then cut his victim's throat and chopped his fingers off with a bolt cutter. Carter hid the body in a forty-four-gallon drum in his backyard before burying it in a shallow grave.

In January 1990 Carter stabbed a prisoner to death in gaol and was sentenced to a further life sentence. This time the judge, Mr Justice de Jersey, recommended that Carter never be released, adding that he believed Carter would kill again 'on the most trivial of provocation'.

In July 1991 Carter led a mass breakout from Queensland's Moreton prison in which eight convicts, including two other murderers, escaped. All were recaptured within days and

Queensland police named Carter as the most dangerous man in the state, if not in Australia.

Frank Carter was thirty-four when he bashed Phillip Harold Clayton to death with a baseball bat. Carter had a long criminal record and was known to be extremely dangerous when he was drunk. He and Clayton had been drinking all day and at a barbecue at Carter's home that night. Carter's girlfriend, Carmel Eva Houghton, told him that Clayton was trying to chat her up. Carter told Houghton to get a baseball bat and asked Clayton to meet him in the garage. Carter then smashed his friend's skull with the bat, cut his throat with a butcher's knife and with Houghton's help cut off Clayton's fingers with a bolt cutter.

Giving evidence at his trial, Carter said that he went into a frenzy after Houghton told him Clayton was trying to 'crack on to her'. 'Carmel said he was trying to chat her up,' Carter said in evidence. 'I was a bit annoyed with Carmel for telling me that... if you say the wrong thing to me any time when I have been drinking, I am capable of anything. I picked up the baseball bat then hit him — I lost control. I realised I had gone too far when I slit his throat. I cannot sleep at night most nights. Phil is on my mind all the time. I just feel so sorry for him.'

The day after the murder, Carter, his brother David and his brother-in-law, Graeme Henry

Savage, stuffed Clayton's body in a forty-four-gallon drum, intending to dump the lot in the river but when they arrived there it was low tide, making disposal of the drum impossible. They then drove the body to a quiet area of Redland Bay, dug a hole, removed the body from the drum and buried it in a shallow grave.

Carter bought garden lime for what he thought might speed up the decomposition of the body. In fact, it worked the opposite way to preserve the remains. This drastic mistake helped the police enormously in identifying what was left of Phillip Clayton.

A massive police hunt — headed by detectives from Brisbane, Slacks Creek, Beenleigh and Ipswich — began for Clayton when he hadn't turned up at his home after two weeks. Almost a month later, detectives exhumed the body of Clayton from its shallow bushland grave. A post-mortem found that Clayton had been beaten to death with a baseball bat, which was later found in the Logan River at South MacLean. 'It was one of the most vicious murders I have ever seen,' said Detective Senior Constable Craig Hintz, the officer in charge of the investigation.

Detective Hintz had begun his investigation after receiving information that a man had been killed by another man named Frank. During the next two weeks, Detective Hintz was able to build on his information and identify the killer and his victim to the stage where the Homicide Squad was called in.

'We still had nothing concrete to suspect that there had been a murder committed — we still did not know the name of the deceased until I obtained information that a Frank Carter had worked with a Phillip Clayton in an Ipswich colliery,' Detective Hintz said.

After Carter was tracked down by members of the Bureau of Criminal Intelligence, police made the arrest. Carter was in a car being followed by police and attempted to elude them by driving in a reckless manner. Detectives believed that they were dealing with a dangerous armed criminal and had no hesitation in calling in the Tactical Response Group. Detectives planned to call on Carter to surrender peacefully when the TRG arrived but Carter had other plans. He took off at high speed and was eventually cornered by four police cars in a busy street. After his capture he led police to the body and was charged with murder. Carter was also charged with two armed robberies and two break and enters.

Carter pleaded guilty to all charges, was sentenced to life in prison and sent to Brisbane gaol, where he automatically became a member of Queensland's most notorious club, the 'Lifers' Club'. He also became one of the gaol's 'heavies'.

After several attempts to escape, Carter was transferred to Brisbane's brand new Sir David Longland gaol in Brisbane, where he planned a mass break-out with a team of other prisoners. When the attempt was foiled, Carter and his cut-throats believed that a fellow inmate had informed on them.

On 26 January 1990 Carter and two other prisoners, Neil Raymond John Aston and Robert McNichol, set upon prisoner Scott Wallace in the belief that he had 'given them up' to authorities. Drunk on home-brew and armed with knives from the kitchen, the murderers mutilated Wallace in his cell by stabbing him about the face, head, neck and body at least twenty times.

Carter was charged with the murder of Wallace and transferred to Moreton prison. While awaiting his trial he planned another mass escape, and this time it was successful. In July 1991 Carter led seven other prisoners up a home-made ladder and over the wall of the exercise yard to freedom.

The escapees included some of the most dangerous men in the Australian penal system. Among them were convicted murderers Adam Vickers and Matthew Randall, who were both serving life sentences, but all the escapees were rounded up within a week. Carter was sentenced to another six months in prison for escaping from lawful custody.

At their trial, held in October 1991, for the murder of Scott Wallace, the prosecutor, Mr Tony Kimmins, told the court that a number of prisoners, including Aston and Carter, planned to escape in January 1990 and bars had been cut in readiness. The plot was inadvertently foiled by police patrolling the prison, he said, but prisoners involved in the break-out were extremely upset and a witch-hunt began to find the 'dog', or informer. Wallace had the reputation of being a dog.

Carter and Aston told other prisoners that they were fed up with informers and that they were going to kill Wallace. On the day of the murder, Carter asked another prisoner, George Lynde, to turn his radio up loud while they 'fixed someone up'. Mr Kimmins said that Lynde had seen Carter and Aston coming back from the direction of Wallace's cell. They were covered in blood.

Sentencing Carter to life imprisonment for the second time, Mr Justice de Jersey said: 'You have now murdered two fellow human beings and due punishment demands you spend the rest of your days behind bars. You are never to be released.'

Francis James Carter is in maximum security in Moreton prison.

11   Kids Who Kill

While most other kids their age were plotting a date, a night at the movies or a surfing trip, fourteen-year-old Bronson Blessington and his sixteen-year-old mate Matthew Elliott were plotting abduction and rape. Murder wasn't their original intention, but it was also discussed and it was decided that, should murder be necessary — then so be it. They talked about it for a week. They even bought a knife with which to harass their victim.

They would abduct a young woman, rape her and steal her car, they decided. The plan may well have started out as two kids playing a game of bravado in front of each other, but by the time the fantasy became reality, a young woman would be dead, many lives would be shattered and Blessington and Elliott would have the unique honour of becoming the youngest criminals ever to be sentenced to prison with the recommendation that they should never be released.

Janine Balding was abducted, raped and violently murdered on 8 September 1988. Her grief stricken family called for the return of the death penalty. The murdered girl's fiance, Steven Moran, said that he would gladly put the rope around the killers' necks. Janine's mother said: 'Prison is too good for them. I'd like to see them die.'

Everyone was asking the same questions. How could such a crime happen? How could a young woman be abducted in broad daylight? What would drive such young people to commit so savage and senseless a crime? There seemed to be no answers.

Janine Balding's fate was being decided on the morning of 8 September 1988 at a refuge in Clarence Street, Sydney, called The Station. It is only a couple of blocks away from where Janine worked at the State Building Society in George Street, in the heart of Sydney.

The Station is a two-storey sandstock building that looks out of place among the highrise office blocks, and boutique solicitors' offices that make up the Circular Quay end of Sydney's central business district. The Station looks as sad and lost as its inhabitants and the bars over the windows give it the impression of being a prison. It is here the jobless, the misfits and the homeless 'street kids' of Sydney society gather for a free meal and some companionship. The Station's clientele tend to live off their wits and to be street-wise beyond their years.

Those street kids who survive their teenage years usually wind up in gaol. But not all survive. Many are dead before they reach adulthood. Drug overdoses, muggings, AIDS and violent death are all part of everyday life to Sydney's youthful derelicts.

Bronson Blessington and Matthew Elliott were street kids. They were regulars at The Station and both were well known to police.

Blessington was the product of a broken home and had a record for stealing. Matthew Elliott came from the working-class suburb of Blackett in Sydney's west and was the middle of three boys. He had been in and out of institutions for years and had an extensive record for arson, false pretences, breaking, entering and stealing, stealing cars and receiving stolen goods. A psychiatrist ranked him intellectually among the bottom 4 per cent of the population.

That morning at The Station when they planned their move into major crime they teamed up with three other misfits, fifteen-year-old Wayne Wilmot, his girlfriend of a few hours, seventeen-year-old Carol Ann Arrow, and twenty-two-year-old Stephen ('Shorty') Jamieson.

Wilmot had been in trouble with the authorities since he was five and was a ward of the state. By age fifteen he had over a dozen convictions for sexual assault, indecent assault, stealing and robbery. He came from a bitterly troubled family background and all attempts to find him a foster home had failed. He made the streets his home.

His new girlfriend, Carol Arrow, had run away from the family home at Leeton, the fruit-growing town in southern New South Wales, a couple of years earlier and had lived off her wits and her body ever since. Her mother would later tell a Supreme Court judge that although her daughter was mildly mentally retarded, she was a loving child who had fallen into bad company.

Shorty Jamieson was an extremely unfortunate human being. He looked like an ape. A psychiatrist had put his mental age as that of a ten-year-old. His long matted hair and Neanderthal features made people reject him instantly. Jamieson also had a long criminal history for theft, sexual assault, malicious wounding and robbery.

When this team got together on that fateful September morning it wasn't long before the topic of conversation got around to crime and Blessington and Elliott told of their plans. Blessington's suggestion of 'How about we go and get a sheila and rape her?' was met with favourable response. A railway car park would be the ideal place to find a victim and the gang decided that they would go to Sutherland because one of them recalled the station having a couple of car parks. It was as simple as that.

A gang of lowlifes who had known each

other for only hours, heading off to a suburb that one of them had only seen from a train window, to abduct and rape a girl none of them knew or had even, as yet, seen. It was so brainless and pointless a scheme that it should have stopped there and then. But hasty and thoughtless decisions are normal in the nomadic world of the transient street kids. The gang of five caught the train for the one-hour trip to Sutherland.

While the newly formed street gang was plotting the abduction and rape, Janine Balding was dealing with her customers at the nearby George Street branch of the State Bank. Everyone liked Janine. She had been at her new job a few weeks, was very popular with her workmates and was engaged to be married to Steven Moran in March the following year. The young couple had bought a house at Wyong on the New South Wales Central Coast with finance arranged through Janine's work. She and Steve had rented the house out and planned to move in after they were married. They hoped Janine could be transferred to Wyong.

Janine had moved to Sydney from Wagga Wagga to live with her sister Carolyn in a unit that their parents had bought for them in the southern Sydney beachside suburb of Cronulla. Bev and Kerry Balding missed their daughters terribly, but they slept easy at night knowing that the girls were sensible enough not to come to any harm. It was a long haul into the city to work every day for Janine but the sense of security they felt at sleepy Cronulla made the journey worthwhile.

Janine would often stay overnight with Steven at his home in nearby Sutherland. When she did, she would leave her car at the railway station car park and catch the train into the city from there. She had stayed with Steven on the night of 7 September.

The gang of five street kids looked out of place on the mid-afternoon train to Sutherland. It was crowded with students on their way home from school and women returning from shopping trips to the city. It wasn't hard to remember the gang. Especially Shorty Jamieson.

Mrs Elva Matyas was on that train on her way to Mortdale and she remembered the gang well. 'They were very loud and vulgar and were threatening the students,' she said. 'The gang told the students to give them their seats or they would bash their heads in. Jamieson seemed to be the centre of attention and he sat next to me. One of the others kept showing him a pornographic book and making filthy remarks about it. They were dressed in dirty clothes and it looked as though none of them had had a bath in weeks. Jamieson talked about going on to Cronulla but they got off at Sutherland as planned.' Yes, Mrs Matyas remembered them well. Later on she had no trouble identifying them from photographs.

At Sutherland the gang pooled their money, bought fish and chips and waited. They staked out the car park on the northern side of the station. They didn't have to wait for long. Just after five o'clock Elliott approached nineteen-year-old Kristine Mobberly as she was getting into her car.

Miss Mobberly told police: 'As I opened the car door one of the youths approached me and asked me for the time. I believe I told him 5.20. As I entered my car, I was asked "was I sure?" I confirmed the time by looking at the car clock and got into my car and locked the door. As I started to drive away, he approached my car again. I rolled down the window and he asked if I had any money. I said no. I noticed he had a yellow-handled knife in his hand. I could not see much of the blade of the knife because it was tucked away beneath his jacket. I got scared and I drove away to my fiance's place at Sutherland, a few minutes away.'

Miss Mobberly and her fiance, Mr Barry Arkley, drove to the Sutherland police station to report the incident. On returning from the police station they passed the same car park, where Miss Mobberly said they noticed a blue/green coloured sedan whose alarm was ringing. A young woman with blonde hair wearing a State Bank uniform was standing near the vehicle.

Two youths were standing near the young

woman, and one of them was the youth who had approached Miss Mobberly earlier. One of the youths had his head down inside the car while the other one was standing behind the blonde woman and appeared to have a stick in his hand. It appeared that the woman was in trouble but there was little that the couple could do as Mr Arkley had a broken leg.

Miss Mobberly said she and Mr Arkley returned to the police station to report what they had seen. Police rushed to the car park but it was too late. The blonde woman, the youths and the car were all gone. The horrors of the night of 8 September had begun. Kristine Mobberly will spend the rest of her life knowing that it was nearly her, and not Janine Balding, who was abducted that afternoon.

Janine's fiance, Steven Moran, wasn't concerned when Janine didn't turn up at his place that night. It was Thursday, which meant that the shops were open until late, and he assumed that Janine had done some shopping and gone straight home. But when he phoned her home the following day and discovered that she had not been home all night, Steven called the police immediately. Janine was not the type of girl to stay out late. Her family were notified in Wagga Wagga. This was their worst possible nightmare. One of their precious daughters had gone missing. They feared foul play from the outset.

On the night of 9 September, just one day after Janine Balding had gone missing, police picked up Elliott and Blessington. A social worker at the Cobham Youth Centre at St Marys, in the western suburbs, had become suspicious of their actions when they called into the centre earlier in the evening. Believing that they had committed some sort of crime, she kept them there until police arrived.

Sure enough, their car was stolen, but Elliott and Blessington had something much more important that they wanted to tell the police. Their friends had murdered a young woman and they knew where the body was. They led Detective Sergeant Sharp and his men to a small dam at nearby Minchinbury that was hidden from the highway by tall trees. In the beam of their flashlights police discovered the almost naked body of a young woman lying face-down in shallow muddy water.

It was Janine Balding. She had been bound and gagged and badly beaten.

An autopsy later revealed that extensive bruising to Janine's body was consistent with where the ropes and gag had been. Other bruises to her face and body indicated that she could have been beaten with a closed fist. The cause of death was drowning. There was the presence of fluid, dirty fluid, in the mouth and in the airway and the lung. The autopsy also revealed that Janine Balding had been sexually assaulted, both vaginally and anally.

Police grilled Elliott and Blessington relentlessly about the horrific murder, but they stuck to their story. They maintained that, with Carol Arrow and Wayne Wilmot, they went along for the ride when the young lady was abducted. Elliott and Blessington said that another street kid named Scott Agius and a man named Shorty had murdered Janine Balding.

They claimed that Agius and Shorty had planned the whole thing. Blessington even produced the knife used in the abduction, saying that he stole it from Shorty to bring to the police as proof. Carol Arrow and Wayne Wilmot were quickly rounded up at Kings Cross. They told the same story.

Police didn't believe them. Blessington, Elliott, Arrow and Wilmot were charged with murder and the hunt started for Agius and the mysterious Shorty. Scott Agius wasn't hard to find. He was a regular at The Station and was brought in for questioning. He denied any knowledge of the killing and had a perfect alibi. Agius was released.

The hunt for Shorty continued. None of the gang admitted to knowing him by any other name and their description of him was vague. On top of which there were fifty-one people nicknamed Shorty in the modus operandi section of the Police Department, all of whom had to be checked.

Under constant questioning, Blessington

told police that the Shorty they were looking for was twenty-eight-year-old Mark (Shorty) Wells, a self-confessed devil worshipper who believed that Satan walked behind him telling him to kill. Wells dressed in army camouflage clothing, complete with a green beret, and on one of his many previous appearances before a court he had asked the judge if he could get the case over with in a hurry as he was in the SAS and had to leave to make a parachute jump.

Wells would also tell anyone who would listen that he killed a priest when he was fifteen by nailing him to a wall. Not surprisingly, Wells had been diagnosed as schizophrenic. He wasn't hard to round up, either, but he knew nothing of the murder and could account for every minute of his time.

By now police realised that the gang had good reason to protect Shorty. None of them had confessed to the murder or would give any further information and Shorty would more than likely give an accurate description of what happened when he found out that he had been blamed for the killing. For two weeks police dragged in every 'Shorty' they could find in Sydney. All the while the name Shorty Jamieson kept cropping up.

But Jamieson was nowhere to be found. The gang members swore that the man in the photos they were shown who looked like a chimpanzee was not the man they were looking for. But police knew better. They had a positive ID from Mrs Matyas who was on the train, and from Kristine Mobberly who was approached in the car park. Police knew exactly who could help them further with their enquiries.

Shorty Jamieson's photo was circulated around the country. He was on the head of the 'most wanted' list. Now it was just a matter of time.

At 8.20 a.m. on the morning of 22 September 1988 Detective Sergeant Roy Wall and Detective Markey of the Brisbane police approached a group of people sitting at a picnic table in a park at Southport, a popular holiday spot just north of Surfers Paradise. On the table were a bottle of bourbon, another of whisky and a flagon of wine, all partially consumed. They called one of the drinkers aside. It was Stephen Wayne Jamieson ... Shorty. They notified Sydney Homicide Squad that they were holding him and within hours Detective Sergeants Carroll and Raue had flown to Southport and were interviewing him.

It was put to Jamieson that he had sexually assaulted, bound, gagged and drowned Janine Balding at Minchinbury two weeks earlier. Jamieson replied: 'No, I didn't kill anyone'. He agreed that his nickname was Shorty. He was then told by Raue that a number of persons had been charged in relation to the murder and that they had all said that Jamieson was responsible. Jamieson repeated his denials, but he was starting to break.

Jamieson agreed that he knew a 'Matthew', even though he didn't know his last name, and he knew a 'Bronson' but he didn't know his last name either. He knew a Wayne Wilmot and Carol Arrow. When confronted with the overwhelming circumstantial evidence and the statements of his co-accused, Jamieson cracked:

Raue: 'Did you rape her?'

Jamieson: 'No. I didn't touch her. I was only with them.'

Raue: 'Would you be prepared to undergo a blood test for comparison with samples taken from the dead girl?'

Jamieson: 'I don't like needles. Do I have to? I did only root her once.'

Raue: 'Where was that?'

Jamieson: 'Beside the car'.

Raue: 'Did this woman agree to have sex with you?'

Jamieson: 'No'.

Shorty Jamieson then made a full confession. He told Detective Raue that within minutes of being abducted at the Sutherland station car park, Janine Balding was being raped by Elliott as Blessington held a knife to her throat. Jamieson said that he held her legs apart in the back of her blue Holden Gemini as Wilmot drove it down the F4 freeway toward Minchinbury.

Carol Arrow was sitting in the front seat, oblivious to Janine's screams for help as she begged her captors to let her go. Arrow was more interested in fondling Wilmot's penis than in what was happening in the back seat.

When Elliott had finished and Blessington took over, Elliott cut Janine's skirt with the knife and forced her to have oral sex with him. When they were done they urged Jamieson on top of the distraught young woman. She was screaming so loudly that Blessington ripped her dress apart and gagged her with it. As they passed the Chatswood Drive overpass near Minchinbury, one of them commented, 'It's a nice night for a murder'.

Jamieson directed them to pull up near the Prospect Caravan Park where he once lived. He knew of a nearby dam that was hidden from the highway. Jamieson, Blessington and Elliott dragged the struggling woman from the car, leaving Arrow to perform fellatio on Wilmot in the front seat. Once out of sight of the highway, Elliott and Blessington again raped the woman and then held her while Jamieson raped her anally.

Jamieson allegedly told police in his record of interview that: 'We all got out of the car. Then Matthew and Bronson had sex with her. The gag had come off. She was screaming. Then I had my turn. I had sex with her. She was pretty worn out by now and wasn't screaming as much. And then Bronson had sex with her again. He slapped her across the face because she wouldn't "buck".

'Then after that, Matthew and Bronson started talking about killing her. Then Matthew said: "What the heck! If one's going to kill her, we're all going to go for a row." Matthew asked me to see what was in the boot, so I had a look and found some rope and gave it to Matthew and Bronson to tie her up. She had no clothes on except for part of her top.'

After she was gang-raped again, Janine was tied up like a ball. Her feet were bound together with five turns of the cord before it was passed around her neck and tightened, forcing her knees to be drawn up to her chin. It was then passed around her knees and tied again. A gag was tied around her face and stuffed into her mouth. If she had struggled she would have strangled herself.

Janine was then dragged and carried over a barbed-wire fence down to the dam, where her head was held face down in thick mud until she was dead. In her left hand Janine clutched a clump of waterweed.

In the web of lies and conflicting statements from the gang members, it was never proved conclusively who actually held Janine Balding's head in the mud and drowned her. But there was no doubt that Elliott, Jamieson and Blessington were all capable.

After the killing, the gang took off for nearby

Mount Druitt, but Janine's car broke down. They left it beside the road and walked. Elliott contacted a man called 'Goldfinger' and sold him Janine's engagement ring while the others used her cash card to draw $300 from an automatic teller machine. Jamieson would complain later that his end of the whole deal was a miserable $30.

The gang then went their separate ways. Blessington and Elliott went to Gosford, a holiday town about eighty kilometres north of Sydney, where they stole the car that would be their undoing the following night. Jamieson headed for Queensland when he read about the discovery of the body. Arrow and Wilmot returned to The Station as though nothing had happened.

After they were arrested, all five were charged with abduction, rape and murder, but the first trial was aborted when it was decided that Carol Arrow and Wayne Wilmot played no part in the murder. They were tried separately for their part in the abduction and the theft of Janine Balding's car and jewellery. Wilmot received ten years hard labour. Arrow was released on a three-year good behaviour bond after serving nineteen months in prison while awaiting her trial.

At their trial at the New South Wales Supreme Court in June 1990, Blessington, Jamieson and Elliott showed no remorse whatever for their horrendous crimes. Blessington whiled the month-long trial away by mouthing 'Get fucked' and other obscenities at the press gallery when the jury wasn't looking. Jamieson and Wilmot repeatedly made rude gestures at the press with their fingers. The public gallery erupted in applause as the jury announced the 'guilty on all charges' verdict after a two-hour deliberation.

Outside the court, Mrs Bev Balding hugged Kristine Mobberly, the girl who came so close to being the victim instead of Janine.

'They should be put to death,' Mrs Balding said. 'I have no wish for revenge. People say that bringing back the death penalty is stooping to the level of the criminals. It's not. Stooping to their level would be to terrorise them as they did Janine. Often of a morning when the van was bringing them to court, I hoped it would run off the bridge or have an accident. They are just like wild animals.'

Prior to the men being sentenced, Bev Balding and her husband, Kerry, campaigned heavily for the reintroduction of the death penalty. In a letter to the premier they wrote: 'Imagine the horror our poor innocent daughter was put through in those final hours. What would you do if it was your daughter or loved one?'

At their sentencing on 19 September 1990, Justice Newman told a packed court: 'To sentence people so young to long terms of imprisonment is of course a heavy task. However, the facts surrounding the commission of this murder are so barbaric that I believe I have no alternative. It is one of the most barbaric killings committed in the sad criminal history of this state.

'So grave is the nature of this case that I recommend that none of these offenders should ever be released.'

Stephen Wayne Jamieson is in maximum security in Goulburn gaol; Bronson Matthew Blessington is in maximum security in Maitland gaol; and Matthew James Elliott is in maximum security in Goulburn gaol.

12   The Granny Killer

On the surface, John Wayne Glover was the type of guy you could leave in charge of your kids or ask to keep an eye on your house while you are away. A big friendly man in his late fifties, he was the backbone of middle-class society. Yet John Glover was none other than Sydney's notorious Granny Killer.

Glover was a volunteer charity worker with the Senior Citizens Society and listed among his friends a former mayor of Mosman, with whom he would often have a drink at his favourite watering hole, the Mosman RSL Club. But Glover's real charity was himself. He would spend the proceeds of his muggings and murders on gambling and drink.

Married with two daughters, Glover and his loved ones lived a contented lifestyle in their comfortable family home in the fashionable harbourside Sydney suburb of Mosman. But it was mainly in these tranquil surroundings that he would bash and kill his victims.

As if to enhance this tragic deception of normalcy, Glover held down a job as a sales representative with the Four 'n' Twenty pie company. His warm handshake and jolly smile endeared new acquaintances to him immediately. He was a walking advertisement for his product. The type of bloke that it was nice to be around.

But beneath that jovial exterior lurked one of the most twisted serial killers in the sad history of Australian crime. A vicious murderer who preyed on frail old women. A bully who forced his defenceless victims into alcoves and alleyways with his superior strength and then set upon them with his fists and his trademark hammer, repeatedly bashing them about the head until they fell to his feet covered in their own blood.

Not content with bashing alone, he would then subject them to the ultimate humilation and gaze upon their most private parts while he removed their pantyhose which he used to strangle them. This final indignity would become his calling card.

If John Glover had been insane then the grief-stricken relatives of his victims may have found some consolation, however minuscule, in knowing that their loved ones met their cruel demise at the hands of a maniac... someone who was driven to heinous crime by an unbalanced mind.

But that was not to be the case. John Glover pleaded not guilty to his ghastly crimes on the grounds of diminished responsibility, but the jury could not accept this. In fact, the jury didn't even think he was temporarily insane at the time of the killings. Instead, they agreed with a prominent Sydney psychiatrist who studied the case and said: 'He built up a pile of hostility and aggression from childhood against his mother and then his mother-in-law. She was the lightning conductor, and when she died he had to take it out on other people. This is a very unusual case because there are very few mass murderers, and most of them are mad, and have an organic disease of the brain. He is not mad.'

As the Crown prosecutor maintained, Glover was very aware of what he was doing. As he killed, he was at the same time planning what to do with the contents of his victims' purses. And Glover was impotent. He was not interested in sex. The pantyhose wrapped tightly around his victims' necks was to ensure that they were dead. But at the same time it would make police think that the crime was the work of a sex killer.

Glover knew exactly what he was doing. Only a cool, clear, sane mind would risk the possibility of being caught by lingering for that extra minute or so to remove the pantyhose and strangle his victim with them. But it was worth the chance to throw the police off the scent.

No, insanity was not the cause behind these cowardly murders and muggings. Glover's actual motives were as old as crime itself — revenge and greed. Combined with cowardice, they made the fatal combination that would keep Glover killing until the law finally caught up with him.

Glover was chronically addicted to poker machines. He would stand for hours virtually pouring money through the poker machines at the Mosman RSL Club. The easiest way for Glover to get more money was to steal it. As police would reveal later, Glover, who was a convicted thief, had a record of cowardly attacks on defenceless women.

After the jury returned its verdict, it prompted Justice Wood to say in sentencing: 'Clearly I am dealing with a prisoner who is extremely dangerous. He is able to choose when to attack and when to stay his hand. He is cunning and able to cover his tracks. It is plain that he has chosen his moments carefully. Although the crimes have been opportunistic, he has not gone in where the risks were overwhelming.'

John Glover carved a macabre niche for himself in the history of Australian serial killers. He was the only one who specialised in old women.

John Wayne Glover was the Mosman Monster. The Granny Killer. And because police had never experienced such a case, investigators had little or nothing to go on. There were no guidelines to steer those trying to find the murderer. If there had been, then Glover might have been brought to justice earlier. The warning signs stood out like neon lights and Glover's name would have rung alarm bells on the computer if there was an established pattern for his crimes. But in the end it was a combination of police diligence and an almost pathological urge to get caught that brought John Glover to trial.

He was leaving clues all over town and, tragically for the tireless detectives working on the case, if this vital information had reached them a lot earlier, then perhaps one life, or possibly two, may have been saved.

When he migrated to Australia from England in 1956, the twenty-four-year-old Glover already had a criminal record dating back to 1947 for stealing clothing and handbags. Almost immediately after his arrival he was convicted on two counts of larceny in Victoria and one of theft in New South Wales. And in 1962 he was convicted on two counts of assaulting females in Melbourne, two of indecent assault, one of assault occasioning actual bodily harm and four counts of larceny. Incredibly, he got off with three years probation.

As in the later murders and assaults, the Victorian attacks were extremely savage and violent and on each occasion articles of clothing had been forcibly removed. Fortunately,

Glover had been disturbed before the assaults could develop into rape or murder. Otherwise his killing spree may have started earlier.

On each occasion the Melbourne victims were violently and repeatedly bashed about the head and body. They were forced to the ground as the attacker frantically ripped off their clothes before their screams alerted local residents who rang the police and came to their aid.

Those first on the scene were amazed at the ferocity of the attacks. The second victim, a twenty-five-year-old woman walking home from a meeting at 10.30 at night, was found on the front lawn of a home. Dazed and in shock, she told police that the man had followed her down the dark suburban street and chased her when she tried to run away. She screamed as he knocked her to the ground unconscious. She awoke on the lawn to find herself bleeding profusely and with her undergarments in a state of disarray. The attacker had fled when her screams aroused the neighbourhood.

Residents reported seeing a young man running into a nearby yard and prompt police action saw the apprehension of twenty-nine-year-old Glover, then a television rigger with the ABC and living in the quiet, tree-lined Melbourne suburb of Camberwell.

Glover said that he had fought with his girl-friend and was emotionally strung out. He was charged and after spending the night in gaol was released on bail the following morning. As he was leaving the police station Glover was stopped by two other detectives who had heard of his arrest. They wanted to have a chat with him about a similar assault a couple of weeks earlier. At first Glover denied any knowledge of the incident, but under intense questioning he confessed to the previous assault and was taken back to the station and recharged.

In light of Glover's previous convictions and the ferocity of the attacks, the detectives were astonished when he was let off with a good behaviour bond and three years probation.

Retribution finally caught up with John Wayne Glover in 1965, but only in a small way, when he was convicted on a Peeping Tom charge of being unlawfully on the premises. He was sentenced to three months in prison but served only six weeks behind bars.

Following his release from prison, Glover seemingly changed his ways and, apart from a minor shoplifting charge in 1978, he would not come to police notice again for many years. However, police now agree that it would have been almost impossible for a criminal of Glover's nature to keep his hands to himself for the following twenty-five years.

In fact some police wonder if Glover could have helped with enquiries into at least five other unsolved murders with similar modus operandi committed between 1965 and 1989.

In Melbourne in 1968 Glover married Jacqueline Gail (Gay) Rolls. They had met while Glover was working at a wine and spirits store in Melbourne's inner city. Gay's father, John Rolls, felt that the quiet, handsome young man was a good match for their beloved daughter. At first Essie Rolls agreed, but it didn't take her long to figure out that Glover may have something to hide.

Even though she was from a well-to-do middle-class Sydney background, Gay loved the gentle English migrant who had arrived in Australia in the 1950s with only thirty shillings to his name. Glover came from a very poor working-class family and told his few friends that he had come to Australia to start a new life and leave behind a traumatic and disruptive family background. With her parents' blessings, Gay and John became engaged and married shortly after.

In 1970 the happy couple moved to Sydney to live with Gay's parents in the comfortable family home at Mosman. Gay's father was very ill and he asked the newlyweds if they would move into the house to keep him company. John Glover was delighted. The poor English migrant with a record of theft and violence had done well. To move to Mosman and into a two-storey house near the harbour was more than he could ever have dreamed possible.

Like all of the decisions in their married

life, it was a joint one between John and Gay to move into his in-laws' home. It was here that Glover's hatred for his mother-in-law, Essie, erupted. A separate wing was built on the house so that Gay and John and their two daughters, Kellie (born in 1971) and Marney (born in 1973), could live an almost separate existence from the demanding Essie Rolls.

Glover would say at his trial that he hated Essie, that the atmosphere was always tense, and that the situation became even worse when Gay's father died in 1981. Glover told the court that Essie was a tyrant. Police had no trouble confirming this when they interviewed staff of the nursing home in Mosman where she died in 1988.

To add to Glover's domestic woes, in 1982 his mother, Freda, migrated to Australia and turned up on his door. Glover loathed her almost as much as he loathed his mother-in-law. Freda Underwood, as she was now known, had been married four times and had had numerous lovers both during and between her marriages. When she tried to move in as a temporary companion to Essie Rolls, it was more than Glover could handle. The last thing he wanted was someone in the house who could bring him undone with tales of his unfortunate childhood. This was the type of ammunition that Essie Rolls wanted.

'It was a shock to the system,' Glover would say at his trial. 'Just the thought of having them both under the one roof was more than anyone could stand.'

At Glover's instigation, his mother moved to Gosford, a hundred kilometres north of Sydney, where she died of breast cancer in 1988. Glover was diagnosed as having the same cancer, although it is extremely rare amongst men. After a mastectomy Glover developed a prostate condition and became sexually impotent. In evidence, psychiatrist Dr Bob Strum said that he believed this to be the time when Glover's life changed. 'It was almost as though his mother was reaching out from the grave and striking him again,' he told the jury.

Despite the family dramas, Gay knew nothing of her husband's dark past and he never did anything to indicate that he was anything other than an adoring husband and father to their two daughters.

The 'start of it all' as Glover would refer to it later, came on 11 January 1989, when he saw eighty-four-year-old Mrs Margaret Todhunter walking along quiet Hale Road, Mosman. He parked his car and, after he was satisfied that no-one was looking, he punched the unsuspecting victim in the face with a swinging right hook and relieved her of her handbag containing $209. As he fled down the street with her bag, Mrs Todhunter called out, 'You rotten bugger'.

Glover went to the Mosman RSL where he drank beer and played the poker machines with the stolen money. Investigating police put the incident down to a mugging and suspected that someone saw the elderly woman with the cash and waited for the right moment. In the drug-ravaged suburbs of Sydney, muggings are a daily occurrence and, while the case was investigated thoroughly, little hope was given of recovering the money or finding the perpetrator of such a cowardly act.

Mrs Todhunter survived the ordeal but was badly bruised and shaken. As it eventuated, she was also extremely lucky.

Glover's next victim was not so fortunate. On 1 March 1989 he had a few drinks at the Mosman RSL after work and mid-afternoon was heading for his car down busy Military Road when he spotted Gwendoline Mitchelhill going home from the shops at a slow pace with her walking stick.

Glover hurriedly returned to his car and tucked a hammer into his belt. Then he slowly followed the old woman to the seclusion of the entry foyer of her retirement village. As she turned the key in the lock, he brought the hammer down with a crashing blow to the back of her skull. He then repeatedly bashed her so viciously about the head and body that he broke several ribs in her tiny jockey-weight frame. He fled the scene, taking her wallet containing $100.

Incredibly, Mrs Mitchelhill was still alive when two schoolboys found her, but she became the Granny Killer's first 'official' murder victim just a few minutes after the police and ambulance arrived. As Mrs Mitchelhill drew her last breath, Glover was sitting in his lounge room wondering out loud to his wife what the sirens in the distance were all about.

Again, the police were baffled. But there was nothing concrete to link the two attacks. There was a theory that they could be the work of the one person, but it was a long shot. Police finally assumed that it was yet another mugging that had gone disastrously wrong.

Ten weeks later, in the late afternoon of 9 May, Glover was heading for the Mosman RSL Club in Military Road when he saw eighty-four year-old Lady Winifred Ashton walking slowly towards him in a red raincoat and with the aid of a walking stick. Lady Ashton had been playing bingo at the RSL and was heading toward her home in nearby Raglan Street. Glover pulled on a pair of gloves and followed her into the foyer of her apartment building, where he attacked her with his hammer and threw her to the ground in the rubbish-bin alcove.

Although suffering from lymph cancer, the tiny and frail Lady Ashton put up an incredible struggle and Glover later confessed: 'At one stage she almost had me until I fell on top of her and repeatedly bashed her head against the concrete'.

Lady Ashton was unconscious as John Glover removed her pantyhose and strangled her with them. Although no sexual act took place, this gruesome ritual would become Glover's signature. And then, as if in respect for the dead woman, Glover lay her walking stick and shoes at her feet before he headed off with her purse containing $100.

Glover later commented to the bar staff at the Mosman RSL that he hoped that the sirens they could hear just around the corner weren't for another mugging. He said this as he calmly fed the contents of Lady Ashton's purse through the poker machines.

Only now did police believe they had a maniacal killer on the loose. There were too many similarities. To date, all of the three victims were wealthy old ladies, all came from the same suburb, all were assaulted or killed in a similar manner and all were robbed of their handbags. This was no ordinary mugger.

Although it was now a strong possibility, the thought of one individual seeking out and murdering defenceless old women was almost beyond comprehension. At the time, police prayed that they were wrong but secretly they knew the truth...they had a homicidal maniac on their hands.

But the chinks were starting to show in the maniac's armour. In a bizarre twist of events, Glover started molesting old women confined to their beds in the nursing homes he visited in the course of his rounds as a pie salesman. This was an aspect of the case that detectives and psychiatrists would later find confusing. Glover maintained that he had no sexual interest in anyone. He never sexually attacked any of his robbery and murder victims. Yet here he was, prowling around nursing homes and assaulting bed-ridden old women.

Local police investigated, but the alarm bells didn't ring. The molestations were not connected to the murders at the time, though at a later date the incidents would play an important part in identifying Glover.

On his nursing-home rounds, Glover first molested seventy-seven-year-old Mrs Marjorie Moseley on 6 June 1989 at the Wesley Gardens Retirement Home in Belrose, which is quite a distance from Mosman. Mrs Moseley reported the incident and said that the man put his hand under her nightie. She couldn't recall what he looked like.

Then, on 24 June, Glover visited the Caroline Chisholm Nursing Home in nearby Lane Cove. He leisurely strolled upstairs, where he lifted the dress of an elderly woman and fondled her buttocks. Moving to the room next door he slid his hand down the front of another woman's nightdress and stroked her breasts. The terrified woman cried out and Glover was questioned briefly by staff but not held as he made a hurried exit.

The incidents were investigated by local

police but were not connected to the murders in Mosman. And it was a long time before it was thought that this information may be of any use to the Granny Killer task force. By the time the connection was made there had been more attacks, more bashings... and more murders.

On 8 August 1989 Glover bashed elderly Effie Carnie in a quiet street in Lindfield, not far from Mosman, and stole her groceries. On 6 October he passed himself off as a doctor and ran his hand up the dress of Phylis McNeil, a patient at the Wybenia Nursing Home at Neutral Bay, the harbourside suburb next but one to Mosman. Again he eluded capture when the blind old woman called for help.

It seemed that Glover could walk in and out of hospitals as he pleased. No-one suspected the pastry salesman. Not once, through that series of molestations, was he ever identified.

On 18 October Glover struck again, and this time with a ferocity that would convince police that their worst nightmare was a reality... that the attacks were the work of one man. But in what would later prove to be a cruel irony, this assault would start them looking for the wrong 'type' of offender.

In the mid-afternoon of 18 October, Glover struck up a conversation with eighty-six-year-old Mrs Doris Cox as she slowly made her way home along Spit Road, Mosman. He walked with her into the secluded stairwell of her retirement village. Then he attacked her from behind, using his entire body-weight to smash her face into a brick wall. She collapsed at his feet. After finding nothing that he wanted in her handbag, Glover left her for dead and went home.

Mrs Cox, an Alzheimer's victim, somehow survived the attack. But she was hazy about the description of her attacker even though she saw him while he walked with her. In her understandably confused state, she thought that her attacker was a younger man and assisted the police as best as she could in preparing an identikit drawing. At last the police believed they had a lead.

To the head of the task force, Detective Inspector Mike Hagan, the new information made sense. He suspected that the killer was a local because of the close proximity of the killings and muggings. As well, police psychological profiles suggested the killer would most likely be a teenager with a grandmother fixation. And Mrs Cox thought that she had been bashed by a young man.

Mike Hagan now concentrated the task force energies in search of a young local who may be acting strangely or had any possible relationship or connection to the victims. Tragically, this theory was only right to the extent it suggested the killer was a local. It would almost appear that some unknown force was protecting Glover, as his next attack would lead police to doubt that the man they sought was even a local.

The murder of eighty-five-year-old Mrs Margaret Pahud on 2 November was undoubtedly the work of the Granny Killer. She was bashed on the back of the head by a blunt instrument as she made her way home along a laneway off busy Longueville Road, Lane Cove. Coronial evidence presented at the trial, indicated that the attack was over in seconds, and from the force of the blows taken by her massively fractured skull, the coroner concluded that it was doubtful that the poor old woman felt a thing. Glover took her handbag and tucked it inside his shirt with the hammer and calmly left the scene.

There were no known witnesses, although Mrs Pahud's body was found within minutes by a passing schoolgirl who at first thought that it was a bundle of clothing dumped in the laneway. As the police and ambulance sirens wailed their way to the murder scene, Glover examined the contents of Mrs Pahud's purse on the grounds of a nearby golf club, where he pocketed $300 and hid the bag in a drain. He then went to the Mosman RSL Club where he drank and gambled with Margaret Pahud's money.

By now police were almost frantic with frustration. This murder was committed about five kilometres from Mosman and their theory about it being a local was losing credibility. Now, they decided, they were looking for a teenager who came from just anywhere.

Baffled and no closer to solving the case than they were when it had all started ten months earlier, the police intensified their investigations. Reinforcements were called in and Australia's biggest task force to ever search for one man was formed. Thirty-five of the state's most experienced detectives gathered at police headquarters and were told by task force chief Hagan that they must work day and night and investigate every lead, however minute, until the killer was caught.

A $20 000 reward was posted by the New South Wales government. Composite pictures of the suspect were left in shops, service stations and newsagents.

Meanwhile, Hagan was becoming a nervous wreck and later said: 'I've had nearly thirty years on the job and I think the worst month of my police experience was November 1989. You get so frustrated with yourself and those around you when you can't get a result and that's very stressful. You'd go home and you're on tenterhooks all night. I wasn't eating or sleeping and this cowardly killer kept murdering frail old ladies.'

Hagan spent most of the day after Mrs Pahud's death at the murder scene yet, as the hours passed, he had to face the grim reality that the killer had eluded them yet again, without leaving so much as a trace.

Exhausted from the lack of sleep by the end of the day, Hagan called into the Pennant Hills police station on his way home to answer an urgent message on his beeper. He dialled task force headquarters. His knees sagged as he was told that they had yet another body... another pantyhose strangling. He later said: 'I just can't explain my feelings that night. To have just come from a murder and to be told there's another one... It was terrible. We'd had two serial murders within twenty-four hours: we'd never heard of such a thing before.'

The Granny Killer's fourth victim was eighty-one-year-old Miss Olive Cleveland, a resident of the Wesley Gardens Retirement Village at Belrose on the upper North Shore. Glover had called there in the early afternoon and, unable to get a pie order out of catering manager Rob Murrell, he left. On his way through the garden he struck up a conversation with Mrs Cleveland who was sitting on a bench, reading. When she got up and walked toward the main building Glover seized her from behind and forced her into a secluded side walkway. Here he repeatedly slammed her head to the concrete before he removed her pantyhose and knotted them tightly around her neck. Glover then made off with $60 from her handbag.

Unbelievably, no-one connected this murder with the attack on Mrs Moseley at the Wesley Home only six months earlier. The task force still had no knowledge of the previous offence. If they had, they may have discovered that a portly middle-aged man with grey hair was in the vicinity on both occasions. There were no clues and the seemingly invisible murderer vanished into the afternoon.

Again the task force was baffled. Surely someone must have seen something? They checked and cross-checked witnesses' statements and canvassed retirement villages, joggers, cab and bus drivers and junk mail deliverers. They even sent a history of the case to the FBI in the vain hope of a lead. No luck.

Sydney's lower north shore was now under siege. People stayed off the streets and anyone with elderly neighbours or relatives was checking on them at regular intervals. Old women were being driven to and from the shops. No-one was taking chances.

And still police investigations continued. The checking and cross-checking went on. A week after the Olive Cleveland murder the police got their first break as the agonisingly slow cross-checking paid off and a pattern emerged. In several of the attacks the victims recalled seeing a grey-haired, well-dressed, middle-aged man. Now the very first victim, Mrs Margaret Todhunter, recalled a man of that description passing her just before she was attacked from behind and robbed of her purse. And Mrs Effie Carnie, who was bashed and robbed of her groceries in August, also described her assailant as a well-built, mature man with grey hair. Both victims described their attacker as an average type of person.

At last police realised that they may have been looking for the wrong man and that their killer could well slip in and out of places unnoticed because he was simply not the noticeable type. Armed with this sense of what the Granny Killer looked like, the police still had to find their 'average' man.

On 23 November another body turned up, the third for the month.

While purchasing whisky in Mosman, Glover spotted ninety-two-year-old Muriel Falconer struggling down the street with a load of shopping. He returned to his car, collected his hammer and gloves and followed her to her front door. As Mrs Falconer was partially deaf and blind, she did not notice Glover slip through the door behind her with his gloves on and his hammer raised. He silenced her by holding his hand over her mouth as he hit her repeatedly about the head and neck. As she fell to the floor, he started to remove Mrs Falconer's pantyhose but she regained consciousness and cried out. Glover struck her again and again with the hammer and only when he was satisfied that she was unconscious did he remove the undergarments and throttle her with them.

He closed the front door for privacy. Then

he searched her purse and the rest of the house before he left quietly with $100 and his hammer and gloves in a carry bag.

It wasn't until the following afternoon, when a neighbour dropped by, that the body was discovered. Although the murder scene was chaotic, this was the first real chance the police had to obtain clues. This crime had been committed indoors and nothing had been disturbed since. They found a perfect footprint in blood on the carpet — their first solid clue since the investigation had begun. However, Hagan still needed to get lucky to apprehend this person who seemed to be able to come and go as he pleased without seeming in any way out of place.

The break came on 11 January 1990, when Glover slipped up badly, but it was a further three weeks before the incident reached the ears of the task force.

On that January day Glover called at the Greenwich Hospital for an appointment with its administrator, Mr Reg Cadman. Afterwards Glover, dressed in his blue-and-white salesman's jacket and carrying a clipboard, walked into a hospital ward where four very old and very sick women lay in their beds. He approached Mrs Daisy Roberts who was suffering from advanced cancer and has since died, asking if she was losing any body heat, then pulled up her nightie and began to prod her in an indecent manner. Mrs Roberts became alarmed and rang the buzzer beside her bed.

A sister at the hospital, Pauline Davis, answered the call and found Glover in the ward. 'Who the hell are you?' she called out, and when Glover ran from the ward she chased him and took down the registration number of his car as he hurriedly drove off. Sister Davis called the police and later that day two young, uniformed policewomen from Chatswood police station arrived to investigate. The hospital staff were able to identify and name Glover as he was well known and popular from previous visits on his pastry round. When the police returned a week later with a photo of John Glover, Sister Davis positively identified him and Mrs Roberts said that it looked 'most like him.'

At last. A breakthrough. But for some unaccountable reason another three weeks were to pass before anyone reported the incident to the Granny Killer task force.

Detectives from Chatswood police station confirmed Glover's name with his employers, rang him at home and asked him to drop in for a chat about the assault at 5 p.m. the following day. When Glover hadn't turned up by 6 p.m. police called his home where his wife told them that he had attempted suicide and was in Royal North Shore Hospital. Police went to the hospital but Glover was too sick to be interviewed. Staff handed police a suicide

note that included the words 'no more grannies... grannies'.

And still it didn't register that the middle-
aged portly man with the grey hair, who was
recovering from attempted suicide after
assaulting an elderly patient in a nursing home,
may be able to help them with their enquiries.
The police returned to interview Glover on 18
January and, with his reluctant approval,
picked up a polaroid photo of him to show
to Sister Davis and Mrs Roberts. After the
positive identification one of the officers told
Davis and Roberts: 'We know who it is. We
know all about him.'

Another two weeks would pass before the
suicide note and the photo wound up on Mike
Hagan's desk. As soon as he saw them he knew
he had his man. Proving it was a different
story.

Head of the detectives in the task force,
Detective Sergeant Dennis O'Toole said: 'We
still had no evidence. If he had said to us,
"I don't want to talk", we couldn't have proved
any of the murders.' Still, the photo matched
the many descriptions of the mysterious grey-
haired, middle-aged man and in his job as a
sales representative Glover could have been
at any of the murder scenes.

Detectives interviewed Glover. He denied
everything. They gave him the impression that
they were satisfied and left him feeling con-
fident that his luck still held. But John Wayne

Glover was under around-the-clock surveillance with six detectives assigned to follow him and find out every conceivable thing about him.

Even at this stage the police didn't have a scrap of evidence that would stand up in court. But in their minds there was no question that Glover was their man.

Hagan had to make an agonising choice. Go in now and let the Granny Killer know that they were onto him and take the odds to not finding any solid evidence that would hold up in court? Or sit tight, wait for him to stalk another old woman and catch him in the act? Hagan opted for the latter. Sadly, it was a decision that would cost another life.

The police didn't let him out of their sight but Glover didn't put a foot wrong. He occasionally stopped to look at old women but his behaviour was exemplary.

On 19 March Glover called at the home of a lady friend, Joan Sinclair, at 10 a.m. He spruced himself up in the rear-vision mirror before he was let in by a woman in a negligee. Observing police had no reason to believe that it was anything other than a social visit. Besides, the killer had only ever struck in the afternoon and only with elderly women. Still, they watched every corner of the house.

At 1 p.m. there was no sign of Glover or any sign of life from the house. The police surveillance became concerned. At 5 p.m. all was still quiet and at 6 p.m., deciding that all was not well, they got the okay from Hagan to go in.

Detective Sergeant Miles O'Toole and Detectives Paul Mayger and Paul Jacob noticed the pools of blood almost as soon as they crept in the door. With guns drawn, they tiptoed from room to room, covering each other but careful not to be caught in a crossfire should the madman leap at them with an axe or a shotgun.

They saw a hammer lying in a pool of drying blood on the mat. As they peered further around the doorway, they saw a pair of woman's panties and a man's shirt covered in blood. Then a woman's body came into view. Joan Sinclair's battered head was wrapped in a bundle of blood-soaked towels. She was naked from the waist down and pantyhose were tied around her neck. Her genitals were damaged but Glover would later deny sexually interfering with her.

It was unmistakably the work of the Granny Killer. But where was he? Was he waiting in ambush? Detective Mayger almost breathed a sigh of relief as he found feet sticking out of the end of the bath. An unconscious, naked, grey-haired chubby man was lying in the tub. One wrist was slashed and the air was heavy with the smell of alcohol and vomit. The relieved detectives prayed that he was still alive. Their prayers were answered.

The man in the bath was John Wayne Glover. The Granny Killer.

After he recovered in hospital, Glover told police of the final chapter in the Granny Killer murders. Glover had known Joan Sinclair for some time and they were extremely fond of each other, in a platonic relationship. However, after he entered the house on 19 March, Glover got his hammer out of his briefcase and bashed Mrs Sinclair about the head with it. Glover then removed her pantyhose and strangled her with them and with others he found in her bedroom.

This sequence of events completely baffled the police. Murdering Mrs Sinclair was in many ways out of character with the other murders and bashings.

Glover rolled Mrs Sinclair's body over on the mat, wrapped four towels around her massive head wound to stem the flow of blood and then dragged her body across the room, leaving a trail of blood. When he had done that he ran a bath, washed down a handful of Valium with a bottle of Vat 69, slashed his left wrist and lay in the tub to die.

But he didn't die and the police were glad of that. They felt that if the suicide had been successful, then there would always be speculation as to whether Glover was the right man. Glover further brushed away their concerns by confessing to everything. Nonetheless he frustrated police and psychiatrists alike with his inability or unwillingness to set out the reasons for his acts. The question 'Why?' was repeatedly met with the same answer: 'I don't know. I just see these ladies and it seems to trigger something. I just have to be violent towards them.'

When he was charged with murdering six elderly women, his wife, Gay, and two daughters, both in their late teens, were stunned. There had never been the slightest inclination that the man they loved as husband and father was the Granny Killer.

At his trial in November 1991 it took the jury two and a half hours to find that Glover was both guilty and sane. Justice Wood sentenced Glover to six life terms of imprisonment and said:

'The period since January 1989 has been one of intense and serious crime involving extreme violence inflicted on elderly women, accompanied by the theft or robbery of their property. On any view, the prisoner has shown himself to be an exceedingly dangerous person and that view was mirrored by the opinions of the psychiatrists who have given evidence at his trial.

'I have no alternative other than to impose the maximum available sentence, which means that the prisoner will be required to spend the remainder of his natural life in gaol.

'It is inappropriate to express any date as to release on parole. Having regard to those life sentences, this is not a case where the prisoner may ever be released pursuant to order of this court.

'He is never to be released.'

John Wayne Glover is in the remand section at Long Bay gaol.

13   The Carbon Copy Killer

Child murderer Barry Gordon Hadlow sat quietly throughout his trial. Even when the jury returned a verdict of guilty after sixty-six hours of deliberation, the forty-eight-year-old Hadlow remained impassive. But when it was revealed to a stunned court that he had committed a similar crime almost three decades before, the prisoner leapt to his feet.

'My life is at stake,' the enraged Hadlow screamed at the judge.

'Yes your life is at stake,' the judge replied, 'and as far as I'm concerned you will spend the rest of that time behind prison bars.'

Hadlow's trial took place in March 1991 and at its conclusion Mr Justice Shepherdson sentenced Barry Gordon Hadlow to life imprisonment with hard labour for the sex murder of nine-year-old Stacey-Ann Tracey in Roma, Queensland, on 22 May 1990. Throughout the trial, the jurors who eventually convicted

Hadlow had no idea that he had been given a life sentence twenty-eight years earlier for an almost identical crime.

When they heard that Hadlow had murdered a child in similar circumstances in 1962, several jurors gasped in disbelief at the enormity of Hadlow's crimes. 'Oh my god,' one of them exclaimed as she buried her head in her hands.

Only after the jury had reached its verdict could the court be told of Hadlow's horrendous past.

On 24 November 1962, at Townsville, the banana-growing and sugarcane town in tropical Queensland, five-year-old Sandra Dorothy Bacon was brutally murdered. The toddler had been sexually assaulted before she was strangled and stabbed to death with a hunting knife. Such a thing had never happened before in the sleepy farming community. The press of the nation focused attention on Townsville. The murder, the capture of the killer and the subsequent trial were headline material for months.

The little girl's mother, Eunice Bacon, said that everyone who knew Sandra regarded her as a happy, bright little girl. Sandra disappeared on a sunny Saturday morning while running an errand for her grandparents. She was from a working-class family and was the second youngest of five children. Her father, Donald, was a wharfie on the Townsville docks. The Bacons lived surrounded by their large family of relatives. Uncles, grandparents, aunts and cousins all lived in the same neighbourhood. On weekends they would get together for family roast lunches. It seemed a perfect environment for a little girl to grow up in.

It was while her grandparents were preparing Saturday lunch for the family that Sandra disappeared. She was running to fetch her sister when Hadlow, a twenty-year-old labourer, called her from the porch of a neighbouring house where he had rented a room for the past three months. 'I'm looking for my sister,' the little girl replied.

'Well, when you find her, could you give her these?' Hadlow called back, holding some comic books in the air.

Hadlow then lured the barefoot Sandra into his bedroom on the pretext of finding some more comic books for her sister. They were alone in the house. Hadlow grabbed the little girl and started to undress her. He held a hand over her mouth as he sexually assaulted her, but he panicked when she started to scream. Wrapping his hands around her tiny neck, Hadlow attempted to block her windpipe with his thumbs. He pressed as hard as he could but Sandra didn't die. She lay motionless on the bed, but she was still conscious. Hadlow then picked up a hunting knife lying beside his bed and stabbed the little girl through the heart.

Police were called when Sandra did not return for lunch and could not be found at any of her usual spots. When a search party was organised, it seemed as though the whole town came to help. At one stage there were over 300 volunteers looking for Sandra. During the search, Barry Hadlow approached the Bacons with some information. Eunice Bacon recalled: 'He came up to me when we were looking for Sandra, but with everything going on I didn't pay too much attention. I just thought it was nice of him to help out when he didn't know us.'

Hadlow also spoke with Donald Bacon. 'I can sympathise with you,' he told him. 'Once my brother went missing for four days.'

Donald Bacon was impressed with the quietly spoken young man who had tried to console him. Hadlow offered his opinions on Sandra's disappearance. He suggested that she may have fallen in the river and been eaten by sharks or she may have been snatched by a childless couple. Hadlow also had a third theory. Sandra could have been murdered and her body hidden in the boot of a car. This turned out to be the terrible truth.

Two days after her disappearance, Sandra's body was found in a sack in the boot of a car at the house where Hadlow lived. Hadlow had fled by then but he had told friends where he was heading. Police picked him up later that day as he waited for a lift to take him up north. He wasn't surprised when he was apprehended and offered no resistance. 'Where have you been?' he asked police. 'I've been expecting you. Yes, I killed her.'

As he was being driven back to Townsville, Hadlow complained to Detective Sergeant Cliff Smith that his thumbs were still sore from pressing on the girl's throat. Smith later said: 'I don't remember everything but I remember he seemed almost proud of what he'd done. In the car he gave us a demonstration. He showed us how he did it. He did seem a bit proud.'

Back at Townsville police station, Hadlow made a full confession. It read in part: 'I sat on the bed wondering what to do with her. She was out of it but not dead. She did not look like dying quick enough, so I got my bowie knife and stabbed her in the heart to finish her off.' After he had hidden the body in the boot of the car, Hadlow took some neighbourhood kids to the movies.

At Hadlow's trial, the prosecution read to the court a psychiatrist's report that said in part: 'There is no treatment for Hadlow's condition and further aggressive sexual offences will occur if he is not kept in a place of safety'.

Police told the court that Hadlow's destiny was decided as a youth. The other kids always picked on him. At all of the schools that he attended, he was the boring, overweight, class dunce and school bully. No-one liked the boy and he was bundled through the education system in the hope that a school somewhere would keep him. Quick to move him on, the teachers were glad to see the back of him. Hadlow was charged with his first serious crime when he was sixteen.

Amid angry scenes outside the courthouse, Hadlow pleaded guilty to murdering Sandra Bacon and was sentenced to life imprisonment. As he was driven away to prison, the angry mob spat at the van and chased it down the street, screaming for Hadlow to be hung.

During his first years in prison, Hadlow was always in trouble, due to the nature of his crime. Eventually the other inmates left him alone and he settled down to become a model prisoner and a devout Christian.

After serving twenty years in maximum security, Hadlow spent the last two years of his incarceration in the low-security Palen Creek prison farm near the Gold Coast. Soon after his release in 1985, he met and married Leonie Moodie. The new Mrs Hadlow had eight children, including twin six-year-old girls, from her previous marriage.

Hadlow had told his new wife of his dark past and she was convinced that they could make a fresh start. The family lived in Too-woomba for a short time before settling in Roma, a few hundred kilometres south of Townsville. Hadlow obtained a job at the local supermarket as a storeman packer.

Hadlow would often get drunk and tell bizarre stories of his prison background. Those listening were never sure if he was telling the truth or not. It was these indiscretions that would lead police to his door.

When Mrs Eunice Bacon read news of Stacey-Ann Tracey's murder it brought back a flood of memories. There were uncanny similarities to the murder of her little girl almost thirty years earlier and the Bacons followed the case right through to Hadlow's arrest. When Mrs Bacon found out that the same man who had murdered her daughter twenty-eight years earlier had been charged, she wasn't surprised.

'Even before anyone told us, we knew it was him,' Mrs Bacon said. 'The mongrel even helped in the search for the missing girl, just like he did when he murdered our little Sandra. I couldn't believe it when I found out that he had been living out in Roma as a member of what I suppose you would call a normal community. I've cried over the past few weeks and I suppose some of those tears have been for the mother of the little girl in Roma. My Sandra's been gone a long time now and the last thing I wanted was for the whole thing to surface again. I believe he should be locked up forever. But then you've got to ask the question: Who's responsible? Him or the people who let him out after he killed Sandra.

'I really knew what Stacey-Ann's mother was

going through. You never forget but you try. It brought back horrible memories. Why little children? Ours was only five.'

After Hadlow was convicted of child murder for the second time, an infuriated nation wanted to know how such a creature could have been allowed back into society.

Speaking on behalf of the Queensland Corrective Services Commission, Mr Roger Pladstow said that Hadlow had met all the criteria required for his parole. 'The law here in Queensland is that someone sentenced to life can apply for parole after thirteen years and Hadlow was not released until after twenty-two and a half years. Even then it is mandatory for anyone who is sentenced to life to remain under supervision until his or her death. Hadlow had been visited in Roma by his parole officer the week before he murdered Stacey-Ann.'

It is now tragic history that the parole officer did not see anything to indicate that Hadlow would strike again.

Mrs Janet Tracey chose to move to Roma from Surfers Paradise to give her two daughters, Stacey-Ann and Elizabeth, aged nine and seven, a better life. Believing that the Gold Coast was becoming too dangerous for her beloved daughters, Mrs Tracey, who had recently remarried, decided the family should leave city life behind them and lead their lives in the safety of a small country town. They had been living in Roma for a month when Stacey-Ann disappeared.

Stacey-Ann was last seen walking her younger sister Elizabeth to school on the morning of 22 May 1990. After she left her sister, she vanished. When the girl couldn't be found by the afternoon, a team of detectives headed by Inspector Bob Pease flew in from Brisbane, 400 kilometres away. At first the detectives feared that the girl had been abducted, but with no evidence to back up this theory they concentrated their efforts on searching the local area. As he had done twenty-eight years earlier, Barry Hadlow volunteered for the search party. Hadlow told police that the missing girl had told him that she was unhappy with her home life and that she intended running away from her stepfather.

Police became suspicious of Hadlow when locals told them of his stories of the years he had spent in prison. They checked Hadlow out and when they discovered the nature of his criminal past, detectives kept him under surveillance.

Four days after her disappearance, the body of Stacey-Ann was found dumped in scrub country on the Bungil Creek outside Roma. She had been partially wrapped in a green plastic garbage bag. An autopsy revealed that she had been subjected to sexual acts before she was murdered. Caught on the dead girl's ankle was a torn piece of paper.

Detectives brought Hadlow in for questioning. He vehemently denied any involvement and claimed that police were hassling him because of his prior conviction. They searched his flat and found a piece of paper that matched the paper taken from the dead girl's body. It fitted like a piece out of a jigsaw puzzle. It was almost as incriminating as a fingerprint and Hadlow was charged with murder and taken to Brisbane under heavy escort. The day Hadlow was arrested, a huge bunch of flowers arrived at the Roma police station. The card attached read: 'To the police of Roma from the parents of Roma. Thanks for a job well done.'

In Brisbane, Hadlow professed his innocence and refused to make a confession, even though the circumstantial evidence against him was overwhelming. He would maintain to the end that the police had framed him because of his previous conviction. Hadlow pleaded not guilty at his trial, where it was alleged that he had lured Stacey-Ann into his car, sexually assaulted her in his family residence and then driven the partially wrapped body around in the boot of his car while looking for a hiding place. The jury of eight men and four women heard from sixty-nine witnesses and viewed a hundred exhibits during the eighteen-day trial before returning their guilty verdict.

Hadlow, who had sat silent and composed throughout the trial, finally cracked. After his initial outburst at Justice Shepherdson, claiming that he was playing with his life, Hadlow unleashed his venom at the police in general and the arresting officer, Detective Graham Hall, in particular.

'It's the greatest travesty of justice since Christ was crucified on the cross. He was crucified with lies too,' he snarled. 'You couldn't lie straight in bed you bastard.' And to the police and warders present he shrieked: 'They'll get theirs. Lying dogs. Their lies will bring them down.'

Justice Shepherdson ordered that Hadlow be pacified, after which, doing little to conceal his contempt, he addressed the prisoner: 'It is quite apparent that a dreadful mistake was made in releasing you from prison in 1985. Your case is a salutary reminder for those members of the community who believe that convicted persons should not be kept in custody.

'From what I read in the press and see and hear of discussions on the radio and on the TV, some members of the community seem to think that instead of sentencing convicted persons to prison, a better course is to require them to attend some sort of therapy course — perhaps sending them to a specified term of listening to poetry.

'It seems fairly obvious that you must have led prison authorities to believe that you were safe to be released. But I suspect that probably one of your weaknesses is small girls and despite having given the impression you were a model prisoner it would be fair to say that as small girls are not in prison, any weakness you had was not going to be exposed.

'I just cannot understand how anyone who had the opportunity of seeing the psychiatric report following the Townsville murder could ever have allowed you to be released in 1985.

'It is my recommendation that you never be released.'

As the van drove Hadlow from the court to prison, Stacey-Ann's mother screamed: 'I hope you rot forever in Hell you evil, evil bastard'.

Barry Gordon Hadlow is in protective custody in maximum security at the Moreton Correctional Centre, Brisbane.